The Pelican in the Wilderness

Iran Chattachnesl

May 2008

Publication of this work has been made possible through the support of the Society of SS Peter and Paul

The Pelican in the Wilderness

A Tale of Adventure and Theology

Ivan Clutterbuck

GRACEWING

First published in 2008

Gracewing
2 Southern Avenue, Leominster
Herefordshire
HR6 0QF

ISBN 978 0 85244 621 8

Typesetting by
Action Publishing Technology Ltd, Gloucester, GL1 5SR

For Rachael

I am become like a pelican in the wilderness:
and like an owl that is in the desert.

Psalm 102:6

With grateful thanks to those who have helped with this book,
especially Angela Budgen.

Contents

The author with a friend

Prologue

Biographies of two celebrities show they had at least one thing in common; their lives spanned the whole of the nineteenth century and this meant that they saw violent changes not only in their nation but also elsewhere. These two men were William Gladstone, a politician; and John Henry Newman, priest and scholar. Their rise to prominence in different fields began in a slow-moving world where travel began with horse-drawn vehicles and ended with trains moving with ever-increasing speed over a network of railway lines. Communication became easier throughout a country which was changing from small towns and villages into large crowded cities fed by the Industrial Revolution. Science brought improvements in health and general daily living although progress enslaved lower classes in factories and mines. A down side was that social changes left little time for religion and God. Such upheavals meant that men like Gladstone and Newman had to adapt or go under.

The twentieth century inherited these changes and developed them for good or ill. Wars which had been waged on a limited scale, now supplied by bigger and better weapons, became massacres which embraced not only the military but also women and children. The splitting of the atom which was hailed as a scientific achievement became a means of massive destruction. On another level, individual lives became less private, family life suffered and the young lost the restraining influence of their parents.

All this change provided the background to the author's life in peace and war. He set out with a simple ambition to be a parish priest but within a few months of his ordination found himself at a tender age propelled into sharing the hardships and dangers of army life. Thereafter he was not allowed to return to his original ambition but was diverted into unusual situations outside vicarage walls where God had sometimes to be shared with Mammon. His constant companions became not fellow clergy and devout churchgoers but those who had still to be touched by the Christian faith yet showed a kindness which was an example to the former. In a way I suppose this book is an offering of thanks to those who walked for a while beside a 'reverend' and shared his laughter and his sorrows.

The Benedictine way of life has been a continual inspiration. Did not our holy father Benedict in his *Rule* make provision for a brother commanded to do impossible things? He may make a gentle protest but if this is not allowed he must get on with it and obey out of love, trusting in the help of God. Perhaps this is a suitable introduction to an *apologia* of one who often has been a pelican in the wilderness.

Ivan Clutterbuck

PART ONE

Chapter One

They Ask for Another

'No peace for the wicked,' my mother used to say when she was not allowed to sit down. I feel the same. Three times retired from navy, school and parish and well into my eighties, I thought I had earned the same retirement most of my friends have been enjoying for many years but I am still being invited to speak at home and abroad and now I am being almost bullied into writing another book. Friends seem to guess from my writing and speaking that I have had a far from usual ministry and they are right. Through no fault of my own I have been tossed about on the periphery of the Church and yet somehow seem to have steered a straight course of sound teaching.

The writing of a new book can be no easy matter. My friend Angela du Maurier, sister of Daphne and a writer herself, used to say it was like giving birth to a baby with all the accompanying pains and stresses. I understand the metaphor although perhaps it is the beginning and not the end which has caused me the most trouble. It is especially so in old age when the walk across the room from armchair to typewriter demands an effort. So much easier to remain on one's backside and let old memories take over the mind! There seems something unnatural for a person of my age daring to start an autobiography and yet, as a friend reminded me, distant recall comes more easily than something more immediate and this gives me a starting point. I can remember fairly clearly an explosion outside our front door in south-east London when I was one year old. This places it about 1917. Later I learned that a Zeppelin had tried to create alarm among civilians by scattering bombs on our cities. Fortunately they were fairly low-powered missiles – more than twenty years later and it would have been more serious and I would not be writing this. A year later, I can remember being stretched out on the kitchen table and a sweet smell sending me to sleep. This was the first of three operations to remove my tonsils, the last being when I was eight and I had good reason for remembering this for they circumcised me at the same time and for days I wandered round the ward of the local cottage hospital with my stricken member wrapped in oilskin. I was comforted by our local coalman, my first encounter and not the last with kindly working classes.

After my first operation I was left to sleep off my innocence and to emerge as a growing boy into a world supposedly purged of hostile elements. As Adrian Hastings puts it in his great sweep of post World War One history.

If the clock could be put back to 1914 bar a few post-war amenities, how pleasant that would be; that was the dream of the twenties society. The unpleasant things had been disposed of – German militarism, the Irish question, Welsh Disestablishment, even the poor. Could one not enter without much trouble into a social Utopia with the help of all the nice things science and progress had provided us?

With confidence the Englishman could sing 'Land of Hope and Glory' and in that spirit I was brought up. My father, a qualified engineer, earned just about enough to give us a comfortable living without too many extras. We had relations scattered round the coastline so I never lacked seaside holidays. I still have a coloured photo taken when I was four where I am holding a bucket over a gentle sea on a deserted beach. This was Clacton-on-Sea where my grandfather had a house. Later this was to become a resort for London East

Enders but in those early days it had yet to be discovered and developed – that blessed word which describes succinctly the overwhelming of our most beautiful spots by a Philistine modern world. But in those early days it was a seaside paradise and we went there regularly until I was eight. Then my grandmother died, my grandfather quickly married again to a lady half his age and my father cut off all connections. The last straw was that he had used his churchgoing to eye the choir ladies, one of whom he took to the altar for a second marriage.

I found all this puzzling because he had always seemed an austere man who put the fear of God in me. I had to earn pocket money cleaning out the chicken shed and walking up and down his legs in the morning to ease his stiff joints. He had spent some time in India building bridges and regaled us with stories of life there but I think he was not there for long – although long enough for him to tell us that curry was so hot out there that it made you scratch your head. Much later I was able to confirm that statement. He ruled the roost over the family and forced my father into following his profession of engineer. Father had always wanted to be ordained but found himself half-heartedly in a career for which he had little enthusiasm. His brothers, my uncles Arthur and Reg, were more fortunate because that were allowed to spread their wings and finally settled in Hawaii where they made money and lost it. They played little part in my life except to send me ten shillings for my birthday and Christmas – a small fortune in those days before the Second World War.

Grandfather did one service at least to the family because after the First World War he subscribed toward a history which was published in 1923, *An Account of the Principal Branches of the Family of Clutterbuck from the Sixteenth Century until the Present Day*. This shows that my branch started in 1557 at Kings Stanley in Gloucestershire and ended with my father. The book was lost for years but reappeared a few years ago. A kinsman made copies of it and I have one in front of me. In addition to a comprehensive list of Clutterbucks through the ages it has a sketch of houses owned round about 1600. There are modern portraits and a copy of a Gainsborough painting showing a fierce-looking Thomas Clutterbuck, land agent to the Earl of Essex.

Holidays on the east coast abruptly ended when I was about eight and in future we went south to my mother's family in Portsmouth. Here life was more relaxed. Most of my relations were in the Navy or connected with it. They were a party-loving crowd, coming and going as the Navy allowed. An aunt lived near one of the creeks which penetrate the port and here were laid up warships no longer needed after the First World War. I spent hours looking at them and picturing the part they had played in winning the war at sea. Now they were discarded and left to rust away, victims of peace one might say. My decision to be a naval chaplain later no doubt was influenced by these early contacts and I never regretted it.

It is one thing to recall to mind people and events, not so easy to relive the silence of everyday life between the wars. Compared with modern life which is noisy in the extreme and where the media is intrusive, my early days were almost mediaeval. For the first ten years of my life there was no radio, no television and very little telephoning. I remember in the mid 1920s my father bringing home a simple contraption of crystal, cat's whisker and earphone and letting us take turns to hear the first BBC programme. After that of course it developed into loudspeakers and the family could listen but entertainment was strictly rationed and we mostly had to make our own pleasures. For middle-class suburban children it was an encapsulating silent world with an occasional social diversion and family life was paramount. I had wonderful parents who made certain life was never dull. We had many friends and once a week at least we went to church. My father was a strong Anglo-Catholic who had been well taught in the years before the First World War and he kept away from all things Protestant. The High Church or Tractarian had had to fight hard in Victorian days to reintroduce Catholic faith and practice into the Church of England and the battle continued in the years between the wars (against opposition from some bishops) to complete the victory. I was drawn into the excitement of fighting for the faith and at the age of six became a boat boy at High Mass, the first rung of the servers' ladder. Our parish church of St George, Beckenham was large with an imposing sanctuary and I remember treading fearfully on the altar steps. It was an awesome experience and I was overpowered by the almightiness of God. Looking back I can see it was an ideal beginning for the spiritual life of a growing boy and since it was balanced by sound teaching in the Gospels, I learnt early the importance of revelation. God was great but he revealed himself in love by sending his Son so that we would not walk in darkness or ignorance. I mention all this because it formed a solid foundation of religious life which I have never lost, even in times of great difficulty and challenge.

So with the help of a steady church life and the example of Catholic parents I grew from child to later life. Last year I had an experience which taught me more about my upbringing. I had to have a serious operation for the removal of a tumour. The anaesthetic was a kind of miniature death and when I came round I was quite helpless with wires and tubes everywhere and dependent on the nursing staff. Gradually I gained strength like a growing child and to the delight of those round me learnt to walk again. But they were not finished with me because I was given instruction about getting back to full strength. How similar this was to the first years of life! So, many years ago I went through this kind of treatment and was given the kind of teaching which has remained with me ever since. Not many citizens can claim this good fortune.

So I began to take my place in the world with plenty of time and silence to read and think. It should be said that like most of my contemporaries I had almost no knowledge of the terrible great war which swept away the lives of an earlier generation. Only now in the twenty-first century have I learnt through television how that war started and how so many were thrown into a military massacre. It seemed that the powers-that-be were ashamed of what had happened and quickly consigned it to history but not before they had erected a cenotaph in Whitehall and decreed a two-minute silence on Armistice Day, 11 November, which happened to be my birthday. As a small boy I remember leaving my toys when the rocket signal went off and standing quietly without understanding the solemnity of the occasion. How could a new generation know the horrors of the war without television or radio coverage and without a rush of survivors to tell their stories in the newspapers? The nearest I got to knowing was through a poor family my parents took under their wing. The husband, a private in the Buffs,* had been badly gassed in battle and quietly coughed his way to an early death, leaving a wife and child for us to help.

'Never Again', became the slogan for the future and in the rare years of peace I did my growing up in a developing suburban world. No longer was I wakened by the cloppity-clop of the milkman's cart or the snorting horse of the coalman's lorry but by an alarm clock warning me to get up to serve early Mass or to prepare for school. I might then have followed the usual pattern, learning, taking exams, leaving to find a good job, marrying a girl from the local girls' grammar and bringing up children. This did not happen and I went in another direction. Looking back now I see that my early training in the sound teaching of the Catholic faith made me want to hand it on to others and the means to realise this vocation somehow became available.

---

* The Royal East Kent regiment

Chapter Two

Swept into a Revolution

Turning the pages of the recently recovered book, *Family of Clutterbuck*, and climbing its branches I can find no outstanding men or women. No Clutterbuck seems to have changed the course of the world or even national history. Certainly we were granted a family crest of 'a stag sejant gules attired or between two laurel branches proper' by heralds in 1662 and confirmed in a warrant in 1787 and as members of the wool trade had our own family cloth mark but that was a long time ago and since then Clutterbucks seem to have spread over the country and even the world, taking their place in daily life without any notable promotions. There have been senior army and naval officers; a Thomas Clutterbuck was knighted in 1689 for being first the Consul at Leghorn then a commissioner to victual the King's Navy in the Mediterranean Seas (he must have been known to Samuel Pepys); there were a number of clergymen but none rose to the purple. Generally they were noted in records as gentlemen or yeomen. I like the latter because it seems to place us among the yeomen of England who served their country well when needed. All would have been moulded to some extent by the times in which they lived and social changes of the age but would not have warranted a whole book to themselves. I am happy to follow in their footsteps as an ordinary citizen and am only writing this autobiography because of the events I have witnessed and in which I have to some extent taken part.

I was ready to go to school in the early 1920s when education in this country was undergoing great advances and since I am writing this at a time when our academic system seems to be in the melting pot it might be useful if I attempt to show how we got any general secondary schools at all. 'Education, Education, Education' is the modern slogan easier to echo than to put into practice. It becomes even more difficult when political correctness and doctrine interfere. So today we have a very confused picture as we try to herd all into secondary education whether they are fitted for it or not. There are some children who seem allergic to the finer areas of learning and are fated to be hewers of wood and drawers of water, as the Bible puts it. This was fine so long as Britain remained a mostly rural nation. Even here education in Victorian Britain was more comprehensive than is generally supposed. Modern research has shown that both in north and south, even in industrial and mining areas, literacy was surprisingly high and that by the time of the Forster Act of 1870 which decreed that all children should have a proper schooling, 90% were literate. This was due both to village schools mostly run by the Church and also to private enterprise, but as the country became more prosperous mere literacy was not enough and the rising middle classes wanted more advanced learning. Already on the Continent countries, especially Germany, were providing technical education and this was to give superiority in modern warfare. By the end of the nineteenth century the race was on in this field and technical colleges and elementary schools were increased.

For parents who wanted broader education for their children, leading possibly to university entrance, there was little choice especially in growing communities on the edge of our cities. Public schools had been the main recruiting ground for Oxford and Cambridge over the centuries for the upper classes and for those who could afford them. Grammar schools often endowed with money from generous patrons had also from early days been a necessary link between government and the governed, ensuring a class of those who could read and write and also setting talented pupils on the road to university. These latter had given excellent service to the nation and continued to do so but they were few in number and often in the wrong place to meet a growing demand, especially in suburban areas like north-west Kent where I was brought up. A new kind of secondary school was needed, but where was the money to come from? Cash was first found from proceeds of a tax on alcohol and whisky under a Customs and Excise Act. Kent Education Committee was one of the first counties to take advantage of this windfall and by the end of the First World War the development of county grammar schools was well in hand. In my own town of Beckenham a local technical college was taken over and extended. Temporary classrooms were put up on the large sports ground behind it and into one of these I entered in 1924, at the age of eight.

Despite the fact that the headmaster and most of his staff were not qualified for such a transformation, the curriculum was quickly widened and I note from one of my reports that I soon started Latin. By 1930 a new Oxford graduate headmaster, Sidney Gammon, had taken over and brought with him a team of well-qualified staff. A new school was built for us and we embarked on a parallel public school future. Fees were low and many middle-class families were happy to choose it for their sons – a similar school was also built for girls at a respectable distance! At the age of eight I won a junior scholarship so had free schooling until I left. Despite this achievement I note from the reports I have preserved that my progress was pretty average, especially in the sciences. However, I passed the London Matric in eight subjects, took up Greek at the headmaster's suggestion and read for an Inter BA in Classics.

I have taken up space to show how fortunate I was to be swept into an educational revolution which was to prepare many for university life and, let it be said, for officer status in the future war. It was not only in learning that we advanced but also in a wide range of sport and general culture. Another dimension was added to school life when Dr Hubert Clifford arrived as music master. He had been conductor of the Melbourne Symphony Orchestra. He not only introduced us to the great composers but taught us to play them. First he started a violin class under an excellent teacher, Margot MacGibbon, whose quartet later broadcast to war-time audiences. I fell under her spell and joined her class where I made slow progress. Teachers of other instruments were also employed and soon we had the making of an orchestra. Instruments were hired cheaply from Boosey and Hawkes so that most could afford them. In the end we had nearly a hundred players and were able to give simple concerts. Dr Clifford wrote pieces which were within our scope. We even entered an international competition at the Queen's Hall in London, attempting *inter alia* a movement from Haydn's Oxford Symphony, I remember. I was never a brilliant performer and struggled along among the second violins but some had real ability and went on to play in major orchestras. One, Hugh Bean (who has recently died), became leader of the BBC Symphony Orchestra. I regret to say that when I left school I gave up the violin, chiefly because reading for the Classics Tripos at Cambridge left little time for serious music. However, I was left with a considerable appreciation of good music and this has never left me.

Before I leave my schooldays I should mention a venture to bring British and German youth together in 1933. Nazis were beginning to rear their ugly head and the name of Hitler was heard more and more. A group of London headmasters felt it was time for the younger generation of both nations to know each other. My headmaster was especially keen because he had been badly wounded in the last war. He had pinned his hopes on the League of Nations but as the years went by began to lose confidence. There was a good response from the German side and by 1932 plans were well advanced with some financial support promised by the government. The idea was that a number of German boys – girls had a parallel scheme – would come to England in early spring and stay in our homes and then English boys would spend a month in Germany in the summer, not in individual homes but together in a country house with a different team of Germans.

My family took part and we were very lucky to have a delightful young man, Rolf Judis, who spoke good English and immediately fitted into our life. In fact he never really left it except for the war years and remained a close friend until he died last year. Another friend was Franz Krusche who ultimately became a Lutheran minister and kept in touch. The stage was set for my first overseas adventure and in the summer about twenty boys from schools such as Tiffin, Alleyn's, City of London, Bec, Archbishop Tennyson's and ours set out for Southampton where we boarded the SS *Bremen*, a fine German liner, for Hamburg. From here we were taken by coach to a small town, Freienwalde near Luneberg, in Brandenburg. Here in a forest a large house had been prepared for our summer school with a team of Germans. This was run on what was later called the Kurt Hahn system. Side by side with our German counterparts we started the day with a run through the woods and a dive into an ice-cold lake, then back for breakfast and a morning of study. My knowledge of German was minimal but lessons were in English, chiefly about Germany's grim past and the wonders of the Nazi regime. In fact everywhere we could see evidence of the nation's rebuilding under a volunteer Labour Corps. The afternoon was given to sport or outside visits and in the evening we sat round a bonfire and heartily sang German songs, some of which I learned later were Nazi anthems – 'Ich hatte ein kamaraden' was one I faintly remember. It was a healthy few weeks with exercise, study and plain but substantial food. Eisbein* and sauerkraut I did not like. I suppose we were given a propaganda drive for the new Germany but we had nothing to promote and looked upon it all as a summer holiday.

At the end of this summer school we were allowed to spend a few days in the home of our original friend who had been our guest in England. Rolf's family kept a delicatessen shop in the middle of Berlin and gave me a fine time. Since they were short of accommodation I spent the nights in a fashionable

---

* A pork dish made from the 'knee' of a pig

suburb with another member of the family. Nearby was famous RotWeiss tennis club and I was given a ticket for a Davis Cup match, Germany versus Romania, in which the famous Baron von Cramm was playing. On Sunday morning I went to Mass at St Hedwig's Cathedral and found myself rubbing shoulders with von Papen, the German Foreign Minister.

I was in fact in Berlin at an important moment of history. Hindenberg, the German Chancellor who had been a member of the old brigade and a restraint on the growing Nazi movement, had died and Hitler was elected in his place. A great rally took place in the central square that same Sunday afternoon and from the very doorstep of Rolf's shop I had an excellent view of Hitler, Goering, Goebels and the rest of the infamous gang. After a rousing speech by the Führer, thousands of brown-shirted men marched through the streets and continued to march braving a violent thunderstorm and driving rain. It only needed the bands to play Wagnerian music to make it sheer theatre. It was on that night that the purge of Jews started and the next morning I passed shops with broken windows and the word JUDE scrawled on the walls. Looking back I wonder why Rolf's family escaped because their name was Judis but no doubt they had proved that they had good Aryan blood.

After my return home Rolf and I continued our friendship and he visited us again. There was a break during the war when he was called up into an anti-aircraft battery. Two or three years after the Armistice we had a letter saying he had survived and that he and his wife and child were in dire straits. We sent food and clothes and heard no more until a few years later he rang from the Grosvenor Hotel in London saying he had come over on business for one of Germany's leading firms. Our friendship was renewed until I heard of his death from old age a short time ago.

There is a postscript to my story. Before I left my German friends I was given a Nazi *Jugend* brooch which I wore as a sort of trophy when I returned home. Some time later my mother and I were having a meal at the Strand Corner House when two men approached, clicked their heels and saluted with a *Heil Hitler!* and a flow of German conversation. I was nonplussed and my mother was scared. Fortunately they left us and I quickly removed the Nazi emblem and have never worn it again. I found it the other day in a stud box.

Meanwhile I returned to my last years at school and worked hard at Classics for the London Inter BA, the equivalent of the later A level exam. Unlike most of my contemporaries I advanced more deeply in my Catholic faith and practice, guided by our assistant priest, Fr Cyril Smith, a Benedictine oblate, who introduced me to the great spiritual writers. If as the Jesuits say, the first years of a child's life are vital for religious learning, then I had it in abundance. There was little Christian teaching at school – the headmaster who gave sixth-formers their weekly ration of religion merely discussed world events – but I had the example of my parents always before me. They never missed Mass on Sundays, said their daily prayers, never quarrelled or used bad language. It was now generally accepted that I would become a priest but how could I afford the cost of five years' training? My parents were not well off and I was not the Oxbridge scholarship-type like some of my fellow sixth-formers, especially after being late in taking up Greek. I might have managed something in history, my strong subject, but as I said earlier I had opted for Classics. This proved a blessing later in life but put me behind competitors in scholarship exams. There were Mirfield and Kelham who trained poor ordinands and even London University for which I was already on my way to an Inter BA.

However, there were priest friends who wanted nothing less than Oxbridge and helped me to apply for grants. My name was put down for Keble, Oxford but also for Christ's, Cambridge where I could sit for a Tancred Studentship provided I was accepted as a member. So we put down the required entrance fee of five pounds – nothing else was required. In the event this exam clashed with the London Inter BA exam from which I hoped to get a county exhibition and I had to choose the latter. I passed the exam, the exhibition was granted, my father contributed money and together with other grants from the Anglo-Catholic Ordination Fund, the Diocese of Rochester, and two City companies I collected the sum of £175 for my first year at Christ's. I really needed more but decided to risk it and full of faith packed my bags for the Michaelmas term in 1935.

Chapter Three

Cambridge, Ancient and Modern

After a few weeks of homesickness, I began a love story with Cambridge and especially Christ's College which has never ended, although modern developments have dimmed my affection. Each college in the University has its own character. Christ's, founded in 1500, was a small college in the middle of the town, known for its friendly atmosphere which has easily absorbed each new generation into its quiet and unassuming buildings. Not for us the architectural miracle of King's nor the vast courts of Trinity, so it was easy to make friends and form groups which would last a lifetime.

Seventy years ago it welcomed a different kind of undergraduate from the present grown-up adults who arrive today after a wealth of experience in the wide world. We had been brought up in an age when a certain innocence remained. Sex received little mention in the media and certainly was kept out of polite company and even out of school life. Growing boys had to deal with the increasing excitement in their loins as best they could, warned only that gaining undue pleasure from such feelings would either land us in hell or damage our health. We were aware of the opposite sex, of course, and fumbled a bit with them when we were alone but were unable to do more because of the watchful vigilance of parents who hauled their daughters indoors if they thought they were getting too keen. Public schools dealt with the insistence of adolescence in their own way but those of us in day schools had to make our own way through the sexual jungle as best we could and were not out of the wood when we left home.

So we presented ourselves at the college gate, waiting to be brought out of sixth-form status into the premier league of academic study – and manhood. Cambridge was an ideal place for growing up in the care of college authorities and especially of a senior tutor who exercised a parental concern for all his flock. It was amazing how our smallest indiscretions became known to him. In those days there were no interviews before being accepted by a college and it was not until I had been in residence for a day or two that I was summoned to my tutor's study carefully dressed in sports jacket, grey trousers and shirt with tie, the essential dress for most occasions. My senior tutor was Mr Sidney Grose who lived with his family in a corner of the college. He was a kindly man who could be fierce on occasions if work was not up to standard: he was also my Classics supervisor. He was a product of St Olave's Grammar School in London and no doubt his influence was responsible for the number of Old Olavians in the college. In those distant between-wars years entrance to the University could be a matter of whom you knew as much as what you knew. Wealthy students could be admitted as part of a finishing course for the upper classes although in my day college authorities were beginning to take a strict line and were sending down those who failed exams. Athletic excellence, however, guaranteed a certain indulgence! To damage the rugger prospects of the University by sending a man down for failure in exams would have earned universal condemnation which few dons would risk.

On that second day I knocked gently on the door, entered and senior tutor and student faced each other for the first time. He must have known something about me from my school reports and no doubt thought, 'This will be a difficult one!' and he was right because, as I said earlier, I had started Greek late. He suggested a programme of lectures and said that on Saturday mornings an hour was to be spent doing Latin and Greek proses in a college lecture room, a foretaste of future examinations. I was very fortunate in my two other Classics supervisors, Mr 'Cherry' Rackham – with a red face – and Dr Arthur Peck, because both were well-known translators of Latin and Greek authors (in the Loeb editions). I suppose I owe much to them because they moulded me into something of a scholar.

More must be said about Dr Peck because he had a considerable influence on keeping me on the straight and narrow of sound Catholic teaching. Christ's at that time was still full of Low Church ordinands, due to the influence of a former Evangelical chaplain who arranged grants for them. I might well have been overwhelmed by them but for a small Catholic guild which Dr Peck had created for each generation. We met regularly for a guild office and a rule of life which meant attending the simple Communion service in the college chapel (still very low) as well as going to the beautiful Sung Mass in Little St Mary's, where Dr Peck was a perpetual lay sub-deacon. He was a great eccentric, a latter-day Dr Samuel Johnson, who made quirky observations on all and sundry. His language owed much to the Classics; for example he would refer to a person whose life was unsatisfactory as 'a great apolaustic'. It could be said that he had not one Bothwell but a number in each generation who faithfully followed him and recorded his mannerisms. Later during and after the war he would at Christmas time send a greeting in free verse which was a kind of commentary on modern life and habits.

Cambridge in those pre-war years was a wonderful place to be. In some ways it was still mediaeval in its rules and regulations. Certainly there were few mod cons in the colleges and although slops were no longer thrown out of the windows there could be a long walk to the multi-seated loo (called the Fourth Court) and to the bath house. I was first in lodgings near Christ's Piece and although we had an outside privy I had to walk the streets in pyjamas and dressing gown to get a morning bath in college. But then the gown owned the town and the hoi polloi had to bow to our needs. You could walk the streets knowing they were mere extensions of university life.

My college was a real family cemented by the strict rule that we all had to dine in Hall each night and what a dinner that was! We were treated to excellent cuisine which gave us a lesson in what good food should be. The main gate was closed at 6.30 p.m. and outsiders banned, including women. So we became a closed community and settled down to our studies. If you wanted real privacy at examination time you could 'sport your oak' which meant shutting the outer door of your rooms.

We had our bright scholars who hoped and worked for a Tripos First but it is probably true to say that most of us went up to get a degree, honours if possible. There was after all so much to enjoy in university life and sport to be played. Although I had to work very hard at my classical studies, I still found time to play games and take part in other activities. I made up for lost time by working hard in the long vacations. In those days the classical tripos was very demanding. It required a knowledge of a wide sweep of Greek and Latin texts in the original. We had no modern technology to help us and lecture notes had to be taken down in long hand. Rapid writing of Greek spoilt my handwriting for life! I struggled with the Greek and Latin prose on Saturday mornings. After two years came the tripos exam under strict invigilation. I did my best in all the papers and waited anxiously for the all-important result. When the results were posted outside the Senate House, I dashed down and was relieved to see I had scraped through.

For my last year I read theology, a poor choice as I later discovered because there were no outstanding scholars at that time. Hoskyns had just died and new talent, like C. H. Dodd, was only just emerging. German biblical scholars were much quoted and phrases like Form Criticism, *Sitz in Leben* were thrown around. It all seemed harmless at the time and I faithfully noted it all down. I have heard it said in recent years that Catholics had made the mistake between the wars of not taking Bible scholarship seriously and certainly it made little impression on me. Had not Pusey a hundred years earlier retreated from dangerous German speculation? In fact, I learnt enough to get the required pass in the tripos exam and so was able to get my BA before going down.

I had grown to love Cambridge life very much and had grown steadily. The strong faith in which I had been brought up might well have been lost in the process but it was not, chiefly because I had Catholic friends who kept me from straying too far. And there was of course the guiding figure of Dr Peck and the church life of Little St Mary's.

I was taken even further along the Catholic way by a priest who had been our rector at St George's Beckenham during the first ten years of my life. He had become vicar of St Clement's Cambridge which was known as very 'advanced'. He was Father Plowden-Wardlaw who was ordained after becoming a barrister and used his legal skills to plot a scheme to make the Church of England a uniate church under papal authority. He was in fact one of the first Anglican papalists together with priests Fynes-Clinton, Corbould and others. He had a small congregation at St Clement's supported by his churchwarden, Dr Arthur Berry, Praelector or sub-Master of Downing College. Fr Plowden-Wardlaw enrolled me and some of my Catholic friends to form a Reunion Society. This was not an ecumenical society but was aimed entirely at reunion with Rome. We met at the Berrys' home in Grange Road and it was here that I met one of their daughters, Mary Berry, who was reading music at Girton. She later became a leading authority on plain song. We became great friends but to her father's great sorrow she eventually became a Roman Catholic nun, was sent to Belgium and was caught in the German invasion. Later she returned to Cambridge and resumed her musical work in the University. We continued our friendship and she recommended me as tutor in liturgical studies for exterior students.

Our reunion society flourished, we had some notable Roman Catholic speakers and I was elected president which called forth from Alec Vidler of the Oratory House, the remark that I was a 'pup fouling my own nest'! My subsequent life dumbed down this tendency but has it surfaced from time to time.

I have discovered that some Cambridge graduates have never returned to their alma mater but despite my wanderings round the world I have managed to keep contact with my college. In the last twenty years I have been drawn into the organisation of the Cambridge Society. This has meant frequent visits and I have found that modern university life is a changed and changing community.

In fact, some of us from the pre-war age find modern Cambridge alarming, like a culture shock perhaps. Think of the streets of old where there was plenty of room for Town and Gown to go about their lawful business. Now there is hardly space for either as visitors from east and west, north and south, fill the pavements and colleges in leisurely droves, flashing their cameras continually. We had foreign students, a few of them, in the old days but never such armies of Japanese, Americans and Germans, all in perpetual holiday gear. This informal dress seems to have been caught by the students for whom jeans, jumpers and trainers are sufficient. Imagine going for tutorials in such casual attire in former days! Even the wearing of a college emblem no longer indicates matriculation but merely a memento of a day out in East Anglia – 'Go on George, have that nice vest with the lions on.'

Cafés, I remember, used to be extensions of college life where serious debate could continue or a man make a rare encounter with the opposite sex. The Dot must have been the scene of many liaisons which ended in something more permanent via a tea party in college (until 6.30 p.m.) and a May Ball. But why spend money on a café today when ladies live on the same college staircase. You cannot get much closer than that! I am intrigued by this new co-habitation. Is it all unisex with differences suspended for a period like those kibbutzes we hear about in Israel where it seems all live chummily and chastely together? I am informed that such continence is not always the rule. A young person today has to take a mixed sexual economy in her stride. Jenny shares a staircase with Andrew and Roger and no doubt provides home comforts for them. A light meal cooked in one's room takes the place of the excellent college cuisine which we all once shared nightly in Hall. It is a sad sight these days to see some college halls almost empty where once they were the hub of family life.

As I have already said most of us went up to get a degree with plenty of added fun. Today it seems a first class is the prime object and colleges are judged by their place on the academic league table. As I compare the old and new generations I conclude that I was lucky to be in the former despite its almost mediaeval lifestyle. It certainly prepared me for the rough life for which I was innocently heading. But that is another story.

Meanwhile, I had to have specialist training for the priestly life and for this several of us chose Chichester Theological College, founded in 1839 as the first fruits of the Tractarian movement. Here the theological teaching was straightforward and the liturgical training complete but my first term was interrupted by Munich and a year later by war. In September 1939 we had taken the place of the cathedral choir who had gone on holiday and were singing Mass when the first siren went and we were at war. This was to change the plans which most of us had made for a parish priesthood and to plunge us into an unknown future. Certainly this was my experience. However everything in my life so far had ensured that my faith was rock-like and mostly able to withstand what was about to be thrown against it.

Chapter Four

Home and Away in Wartime

A Short Curacy

The Devout Life by St Francis de Sales had been early reading
in my young church life. In the chapter 'Devotion is Suited to
All vocations and Professions' the saint writes, 'Devotion
ought to be practised differently by the gentleman, by the
artisan, by the servant, by the prince, by the widow, by the
daughter, by the wife; and not only so but the practice of
devotion ought to be accommodated to the strength, to the
affairs and to the duties of each one individually'. It was the
duty of a parish priest to be able to minister to each situation.

This advice was helpful in my first parish on the fringe of
London. The church of Holy Trinity, Lamorbey in north-west
Kent was the last parish in the Rochester diocese and was a
typical village building. High Church vicars had gently
adapted it for Catholic worship as far as the local gentry
would accept. Between the wars a large number of people
from the East End of London were transplanted into this countryside and housed in new housing estates, making it an extension of suburbia. Some brought with them the Catholic faith
and practice they had been taught by priests in the great slums.
So there was a merging of old and new and the clergy had to
minister to both.

When war broke out the vicar was Father Laurence Barrett,

one of three brothers who were priests in the Catholic tradition. He had served in notable London parishes but had recently married a society lady and brought her to his suburban vicarage. She was unused to housework so the house suffered and mice could be seen running wild and unmolested. The parish needed a curate and Fr Barrett came to Chichester to find one. Since I was a Rochester ordinand, the lot fell upon me . . . I had only done half of my training but since I had read Classics and theology at Cambridge, I was considered safe to be launched in to a parish. Just after my twenty-third birthday, the minimum age required, I was made deacon on 17 December in the first Advent of the war and clutching a suitcase and gas mask arrived by bus in the blackout at my parish. The vicarage was not thought to be a suitable lodging for me so I was lodged with a family in a chalet bungalow, part of a housing estate, and I was well looked after despite the rationing which was beginning to grip the nation.

The war had not begun in earnest and I was able to walk into a normal life with a daily Mass and plenty of social activity. Both suited me very well and I was soon accepted especially by the young. Here perhaps I should say a bit more about myself. Although my parents were good church people, the rest of our relations were not, nor was there a recent tradition of clergy in either branch of the family. There was no religious background in my school life nor in most of the friendships I had. We wore our Christian faith sensibly and quietly and did not try to intrude it into the non-religion around us. So you might say I early learnt to live in two worlds, the religious and the worldly and was accepted by both. I liked parties and dancing and, I suppose, was considered a social asset by mothers who let me partner their daughters. I even enjoyed planting a kiss on one as a mini-conquest, the limit of sexual advances in those days! Looking back over my life I have to confess to continuing that life in two worlds and have been able easily to change from one to the other. I also have come to learn that I have the gift of empathy which of course is deeper than sympathy and enables one to enter into the very thoughts of another. Whether the great spiritual writers of the past would have agreed with this living in both worlds, I do not know but the widening gap between the Church and the world has made this almost inevitable for a priest with mission in mind.

All this was in the future and meanwhile I had to learn to be a good parish priest. I was lucky in my vicar who trained me very well. Every afternoon I was sent out, clad in black suit, black hat and shoes, in clerical collar and with rolled umbrella to visit families house by house. I had learnt that a house-visiting clergy meant a church-going people, and I have always found that to be true up to the present day. I had to report back to the vicarage at the end of the day. Life flowed on quietly until the war erupted into violence in the middle of 1940. One Saturday afternoon at the beginning of September as I was setting out on my afternoon visits I looked up and saw what looked like a flight of large black birds. The German bombers wheeled left and, following the Thames, attacked oil installations and set them on fire. After dark they returned guided by the flames which we could see lighting up the sky. This was the beginning of the Blitz which sent us seeking cover in the months ahead. Sidcup was on the fringe of London but became the flight path to the city and regularly received random bombs. Life suddenly became dangerous for everybody. Through the winter I made my way to early Mass with explosions not far away and daily life often disrupted. I remember taking a funeral in the local churchyard when the sirens sounded. 'What shall we do?' I asked the undertaker. 'I know what I shall do,' he replied. 'I shall jump into the empty grave.'

The city of Rochester, which was close to Chatham dockyard, received regular attention and the Cathedral was too dangerous for my priesting in Advent. So we were moved to Oxford by the new Bishop Christopher Chavasse, an Evangelical. In the bleak church of St Aldate's the bishop laid his hands on my head and I was made a priest, the fulfilment of my hopes since I was a boy. If the liturgy was minimal I could console myself with the thought that the Bishop was within the apostolic succession. It was 22 December 1940 and I immediately dashed back to my parish to say my first Mass on the next day. Enemy activity was at its height and a number of us took refuge in a spinster's house, sleeping on the floor. So early on the next day we all made our way to church and I offered the Holy Sacrifice for the first time. The second Christmas of the war followed and I was able to cycle home for a brief celebration with my parents.

My vicar then announced that he had been offered a living in Lincolnshire and departed with his wife, leaving me in charge to look after Lent and Easter. Given a free hand and well supported I introduced what had been missing so far in worship. When the new vicar arrived it quickly became clear that I did not enjoy his support, so sought the advice of the new Master of Christ's, Canon Raven who thought that I would do well as chaplain of Marlborough. I then had to face my very Low Church bishop who said, 'You are not going to Marlborough but into the Army as chaplain to learn better manners.' Churchmanship manners, no doubt.

I could have refused, I suppose, because I was four years too young for army service, but it seemed exciting to follow most of my contemporaries into action. Looking back the bishop was irresponsible. A young priest needs at least three years to complete his training and here I was only six months after ordination, and very young at that, being cast to the lions of seasoned unbelief.

My grooming as a respectable Anglican clergyman began without much delay. My black suit was stripped from me and I was clothed in khaki by a Bond Street tailor, then given three pips. No longer Father but an officer with the King's commission I was promptly saluted by soldiers as I stepped out of Wetheralls. I was then sent to an Army Chaplains' training school at a college in Chester and with a mixed class of new chaplains shown how to behave inside and outside church to please the Establishment, in church surplice and stole instead of Mass vestments. Then I was sent to a large training depot at Blackdown Garrison, not far from Aldershot. This had been built regardless of expense by Hore Belisha – a war minister before the war. The officers' mess was entered through Georgian pillars and inside all was comfort; a civilian messman ensured the food was good and it all gave the appearance of a gentleman's club. In fact, as the Army was still recovering from Dunkirk, retired officers had been called back to help with training and now released from married life found themselves available for an increasing number of ATS officers who had resigned themselves to spinsterhood. Tennis and cricket was played and altogether it seemed far from the war. Parties were regular and I was taken under the wing of a middle-aged Irish officer who made sure I was not lonely!

There were several regiments training in the garrison, each with his own chaplain and all met in the garrison church on Sunday mornings for a parade service, Mangled Mattins, at which I took my turn at preaching. I was given part of the barracks which received new recruits who arrived weekly. I had to interview each Church of England man and ask about his religion. This was mostly nil and I began to get a picture of my fellow countrymen which had been hidden from the parish clergy. For the few churchmen I was able to provide a simple Communion in a makeshift chapel, not for the last time in my army career. I was able also to offer another service for I noticed that a number of men who arrived had theatre and orchestra experience, some from well-known dance bands. So I suggested to the entertainment officer that we might form our own concert party, arranging for them to be diverted from other duties. We soon had a professional cast and as far as I know they stayed on to provide fun for those far from home.

Within a few months, I had been transformed into a life where liturgical meant nothing and army discipline was all. The War Office was God and the diocesan bishop meant nothing. Chaplains were moved around to look after the growing army and had to make the best of a bad job. I was sent to a battalion of the Buffs in east Kent who were guarding airfields in case of invasion. Regional headquarters was billeted in a crumbling country house belonging to Lord Hothfield. I had few facilities for my job which was travelling round the RAF stations where the standard of living was higher than ours! I had to rig an altar where I could find a flat surface and celebrate with a minimum of fuss. It was in the Buffs that I learnt more about the religious state of my soldiers. They just had none and when I tried to teach them I was shouted down, an experience I have remembered all my later life.

I was physically very fit with regular route marches and five-mile cross-country runs but the strain of trying to adapt to the conditions affected me and I was moved on finally to an army boys' school near Reading where I taught daily and loved it. It was here that I met and married my wife, an ATS officer. A word might be said about marrying in wartime. In 1942 there was a fine balance between victory and defeat and nobody knew what the future would hold. This, I suppose, made some of us grab at immediate possibility without thought for the morrow. In some cases this ended in marital disaster when normal life resumed but in my case somehow it has held together into old age.

In my first year as a chaplain I served in a variety of units, even doing a brief spell in the Army's cathedral, the Royal Garrison Church in Aldershot. Perhaps the authorities did not know what to do with the youngest chaplain in two great wars. If so, it was strange that I was appointed to the 4 CCS, a mobile hospital in the heart of Kent which, it was whispered, was preparing for a paratroop operation deep in the heart of Yugoslavia. It was a wild idea of Winston Churhchill to make some kind of gesture in south-east Europe. It had little chance of success and was finally dropped. Meanwhile surgeons, doctors, even a dentist, orderlies and three chaplains mustered in a medical centre at Benenden School – the girls had been evacuated – and awaited orders. A vague, hesitant regular Royal Army Medical Corps (RAMC) colonel was in charge who for want of anything else to do gave us a programme of cross-country runs and route marches, no doubt to make us fit for keeping up with the rest of the military. It was suggested that the chaplains should be given the sight of blood and all three of us stood round an operating table while one of the surgeons opened up a patient who had appendicitis. The Church of Scotland chaplain, Joe Easton, immediately passed out and had to be removed but the Roman Catholic chaplain, Fr Copsey, and I watched with interest. It was in fact, useful experience for what was to come later.

The message finally came through that the paratroop operation was off and we settled down to await further orders. Meanwhile we opened up as a general hospital and were joined by army nurses. It also gave doctors and chaplains a chance to get to know each other. An easy relationship was built up where each respected the other's role in illness. Before the war they had been highly respected medical men and two of the surgeons were at the height of their profession. I also found some good churchmen among the orderlies and was rarely short of a congregation at Communion. One, Ken Daniel, was ordained after the war. Christmas came, then a glimmer of spring and suddenly it was all activity. We were put on a troop train at Cranbrook and taken round London north to Otterburn in the depths of Northumberland. It was an early Easter in 1943 and snow was on the ground. Officers were billeted in a large empty house without heating. Holy Week was lost in all this activity but I celebrated Easter simply for the large number of men in their encampment. Our next move was to an empty house at Bothwell on the edge of Glasgow and when we saw that all the ambulances had been waterproofed, we began to feel we were due for a big adventure.

cho

At this point, I no longer have to rely on a long memory because I found among my papers a yellowed account of what followed. I must have written it when I was safely home. We were apparently taken on a short train journey round Glasgow to a quayside on the Clyde and looking out from our carriage windows we had our first view of a number of grey-painted ships at anchor in the harbour. There had been much speculation about the 'big ship' which we were going to catch but at times it seemed as if we were not booked for it at all. The issue of tropical kit started tongues wagging again and every destination was mentioned from the coast of France to the shores of Burma.

Batmen always seemed to be the best-informed members of our CCS but they swore they learnt all their 'gen' from the cooks in the kitchen!

Now there was no doubt we were due for a sea trip. Men began to struggle awkwardly out of the carriages – they were weighed down by their webbing equipment which they wore with difficulty because RAMC personnel do not expect to travel like frontline soldiers. I had a little more to carry than the rest because in addition to the suitcase allowed to officers I had an expanding case containing church equipment. It was hard to decide what to take within the very limited weight allowed, for we were leaving England not for a short cruise but maybe for years. If ever an Anglican priest had to make decisions about fundamentals I had to do so in my last few days ashore. Finally I was left with my Communion case packed to the limit with crucifix, chalice, candlesticks, reversible burse and veil, pyx, wafers and pocket missal. This small case fitted into the larger suitcase and left room for cassock, surplice, two stoles and a lightweight altar frontal. This last proved invaluable because it gave the appearance of a church whenever I fitted it to the front of a table or packing case.

I made my way with greater difficulty than the rest into the tender which was to take us to our transport ship, the *Dunnator Castle*. Assault craft could be seen strapped to its side and this warned us that we should not be disembarking leisurely at some port but would arrive informally at some foreign beach. In contrast to any sworn secrecy our embarkation was strangely public. Crowded passenger steamers wandered through the harbour and people strained their eyes to see what was going on. It was some days later, however, when we began to move slowly towards the mouth of the river. Early summer dusk was falling when we noticed the shore disappearing and we headed for some unknown foreign land.

After a few farewell cheers the troops resumed a game of 'housey-housey'. One or two remained at the rail and gazed at the receding land wondering when, if ever, they would see their country again. They were leaving behind a way of life, companions, scenery they had known from birth. Day after day before the war life had followed the same routine, breakfast, work, home, cinema or wireless, bed, the same faces and buildings marking a regular way of life. It was now goodbye to all that and in future the Army would decide our lives. There was, of course, excitement at the thought of a change of routine but already many had shared our position for foreign service and never returned. Here was I, a parish priest for only a short time, leaving a safe haven behind a vicarage wall and now sharing the common life, about to go into battle, wearing the same kind of clothes and eating the same rations. There came alive for me once more on that June evening a sense of vocation which is felt too seldom in the life of a minister of Christ. Did not Saint Paul have the same feeling as he left Palestine and headed for strange lands to preach where God willed and to return when God allowed it? I had a high expectation of drawing men to Christ and administering the sacraments on the battlefield to dying men. It did not turn out that way but at least the thought was there.

We steamed steadily out into the Atlantic with occasional warnings that U-boats were at large but we were well escorted by the Navy. Our day was marked by meals, boat drill and Physical training (PT). I was able to say Mass daily in the Commanding Officer's day cabin and men came in twos and threes.

We did not know our final destination although some had narrowed it down to Sicily or Crete. Then when we were in mid-ocean the Commanding Officer mustered us all on deck and read out the secret instructions which had just been opened. We were on our way to join the Eighth Army in the invasion of Sicily and cheering greeted the announcement. From that moment maps were produced and lectures given on the type of country before us. None had been on a combined operation before and we all imagined it would be a desperate venture.

Our convoy changed course and we were soon in a warmer climate. We passed Gilbraltar by night and hugged the African coast. The sea turned to a vivid blue and the sun overhead scorched us as we sat or exercised on deck. On the Sunday before the attack there was a church parade with an order used by order of General Montgomery. This was my first contact with the religious background which the Army Commander had brought to his men. There were four chaplains on board our ship, two Anglicans, a Roman Catholic and a Presbyterian. We held our services in different parts of the ship and I remember facing more than a thousand men in the stern. My sermon was created round the words which the Commanding Officer had used in his first instructions to us about ship behaviour: 'We are all in the same boat'. I reminded them that many years before a boatload of men had been caught in a storm on the Sea of Galilee in Palestine and in their panic they had turned to one who was asleep in the stern, our Lord Jesus Christ. He had calmed the sea and rescued his followers from distress. In our present venture we had the same person near us to listen to our prayers and he would not desert us.

These words of mine no doubt would have been useful to a shipload of Christians but in those days I had not yet plumbed the depths of human ignorance. My optimism was not increased when, just before landing, only fifty from the whole ship came to their Communion.

We stopped in Algiers Bay for a few hours and had a brief look at land. We also saw two battleships obviously ready to sail. By nightfall we were at sea waiting for news of the first landing in Sicily. Next morning we heard on the wireless that the landing had been successful and knew that soon it would be our turn.

Chapter Five

The Third Wave and After

Many years after the war I was invited to preach at a church festival in the west country and drove at some speed from London and, late, found the village, parked the car, threw open the church door and found nobody inside; complete anticlimax. The venue had been changed.

Early on 13 July 1943 before Homer's early morning rosy-fingered dawn had lightened the sky, we all gathered on our troop ship's deck in full battle kit and waited to be taken ashore. The ship's engines had stopped and we drifted slowly towards a sandy beach. In the night we had heard a rumble of guns and saw tracer bullets soaring into the sky and wondered what awaited us. Assault craft were lowered and clumsily in our equipment we went over the side and soon were vomited onto the beach. In the morning light we found nothing there and heard nothing except a few land mines exploding under the feet of unwary soldiers.

It was an anticlimax and remained so for the next few days. There were no bodies for the doctors and chaplains to work on and it became very hot indeed. It seemed we were on Pacino beach which had been quickly taken by our advanced troops who then chased the enemy inland. We could not follow because our ambulances and other transport had not been landed. So surgeons, doctors, medical staff and chaplains dug foxholes in the sand and awaited orders. Evening came and we were still there, targets for mosquitoes and Stuka bombers. I eased myself further into my sandpit and spread my white mosquito net over me until it was realised that they could be seen from above. So we remained unprotected and no doubt became victims of the malaria-bearing insects, if not of German soldiers. It is worth noting at this point the effect on hygiene of thousands of men answering the call of nature on the local vegetation. The problem would remain throughout the campaign in a still primitive country and even later in the city of Naples our occupying army soom reduced the plumbing to chaos. It may now seem a minor matter but the danger to health in flaming hot weather can be imagined and dysentery and jaundice soon took their toll in addition to malaria. It was not only the surgeons who were kept busy.

On the second day we moved into a small village and were joyously received by the local people who were short of everything: food, water and doctors. One of the first duties of our unit was delivering a Sicilian woman of her baby. My first was to bury two Canadian soldiers who had died from alcoholic poisoning – they had sampled too well the local Marsala wine. Funerals were to become a regular duty and in many cases meant using old cemeteries. Since the hard ground made it impossible to dig graves, it was the custom to bury people above ground in plaster compartments. The smell of death was overwhelming but a local priest showed me the answer. On entering the cemetery he plucked a flower and held it to his nose and this helped my sensitive nose.

Our transport had now been unloaded and we set off for the front line in the middle of the island. The RC chaplain and I however were detailed to take a burial party to a forest area near Syracuse where a lorryload of Buffs had been blown up. Parts of bodies were scattered among the trees and we had first to try to identify the men from their name discs, then make a list, finally to bury then in the hard ground. It was baking hot and we sweated profusely. The job done we rejoined our CCS which was taking shape under canvas in an olive grove. Once the beds had been put up the wounded arrived because the fighting had become intense and soon our surgeons were working day and night to patch up the wounded and send them back by ambulance to a hospital ship. The dying were made comfortable and these became my special care. My sound teaching as a priest left me in no doubt that the Last Sacraments of forgiveness and Communion should be offered to those who needed it and a few of us quickly improvised an altar from a packing case in a small tent. Here I was able to say Mass. It was a sadness that few of my Anglican patients knew what they wanted; in fact few had been taught the Christian faith at all and it was too late to start teaching them. Most anyway were so drugged that they were only partially conscious. Still I did my best. It was clear from my contact with other Anglican chaplains that few had been trained for such emergencies and were content to be little more than welfare officers who provided comforts for the troops. There was one chaplain in my army training course who had never celebrated Holy Communion whom we had to teach at the last minute! Within a week he had been let loose among the troops! Back at the war I remember that a captured German soldier had been operated on for appendicitis. It was successful but he slowly killed himself by tearing off the dressing and he kept shouting *Heil Hitler* until his voice became faint and he died. A certain faith there!

At last German resistance ended and they were pushed off the island. We had time to look around us at the local Italian situation and noticed a number of young men who had obviously taken little part in the fighting. We also became aware of young women who were offering themselves to our men in exchange for food and money. This was surprising because we had been warned before landing about strict Roman Catholic teaching on sex and we were told to keep off the women. Now we had a problem of keeping the women off our men! In fact venereal disease began to land troops in hospital and later when the army reached Naples the problem became serious as men sought relief from the horrors of the Cassino fighting. In one place in Sicily small children were sent to bring our men to brothels and it became necessary to preach sermons against immorality. During my visits to local cemeteries to bury the dead I was able to raise the problem with a local Dominican monk. He explained that the shortage of food and other necessities of life made women do anything to get them. Also he said that the temperamental southern character had been completely bowled over in their country's change of fortune. They had been promised a cheap and easy victory by Mussolini and had thought the British and French to be completely defeated. Instead of glory they had been invaded, their country turned into a battleground and their leader forced to abdicate. All was lost and all that remained was to make as much as possible for themselves while they could.

I have indicated earlier in this book the difficulties a young army chaplain, and I was the youngest in two great wars, had to overcome to carry out his priestly duties. Now following an advancing army in a foreign country it became even harder. At times there was little for him to do except be carried with the rest in the back of an uncomfortable three tonne lorry. My impression of the first weeks is of being very hot and sweaty, covered with dust and flies and able to hold very few services. It was only by using a few faithful other ranks that I was able to say Mass at all. Above all my memories are of winding, primitive roads. They were obviously not made for modern traffic and were a great danger to our men. One of our hospital lorries fell off a cliff killing one of our doctors, a nice man called Levick who was one of a few showing any sign of religion at all. I was beginning to be fed up at such an irregular and uncertain life when I went down twice with malaria, an unpleasant disease but not altogether surprising since we had been exposed continually to mosquitoes. When I emerged from hospital I found myself at Eighth Army HQ on the beach at Messina, the Germans having been pushed out of Sicily. I spent several pleasant days with the Assistant Chaplain General, Hughes, and his staff chaplain, John Waddington, before setting out to join my new unit – the 78th Field Regiment – which was already pushing up the east coast of Italy chasing the enemy. My first stop was at a transit camp, a little north of the toe of Italy. This camp had a skeleton staff whose job was to send detached men up the line to their units.

However I noticed that a number were not anxious to move on! Next morning, since I was the only officer, I was placed in charge of two lorryloads of men and we drove through rough country to the next camp on the foothills of the Appenines. Here my new batman, Tod Milton, was awaiting me with my small truck and we were soon at the RHQ of my new unit. Although it was an Edinburgh Territorial Army regiment it had lost most of its Scots in the desert campaign. The CO was 'Tishy' Benson, a typical ride-to-hounds English officer, whose first question was 'Do you play bridge?' Fortunately I did and passed the first test. My job was to visit the different batteries and offer my services. There were not many takers and once again I had to scrape together a quorum for Mass. The enemy was not far ahead and constantly put us under fire. Here began a strange chain of events. On my way to a stricken battery an enemy shell exploded beside me throwing me to the ground. I appeared unhurt and continued to encourage some very frightened men. I shall never forget the look of abject fear on their faces as the shells rained down.

We pushed on up the slopes of the Appenines, enduring some very wintry weather. I slept under a small bivvy and wakened one morning to find the tent embedded in snow. Two of our best officers, one a rugger international, were killed in a minefield which surrounded us. After Christmas we were moved to Naples on the west coast and drove into the sun and a warmer climate. We were billeted in a suburb, the officers in a villa, and quickly overloaded the sewage system! In the few days' rest I was able to sample some civilised delights: a symphony concert in the fine opera house and a meal at the naval base with fine food and white tablecloths!

After too short an interval we were moved up to join the battle of Cassino and put up the heaviest barrage of the war. Later I paid a visit to some sick men in the military hospital at Caserta and suddenly felt very ill and unable to climb stairs. Fortunately a medical specialist was at hand who was a good churchman. He heard my history and said, 'You have been in the Army almost three years and you are still too young, apart from having been blown up by a shell. I shall admit you to hospital.' So it happened that from hospital I was passed on to a comfortable convalescent home in Sorrento, then to Algiers in North Africa in a hospital ship, finally being discharged in 1944 and shipped back home. The Army classed me as B and since I was unfit for the Second Front invalided me back into civilian life – all within a few months. I was never told my actual diagnosis and can only guess that someone wanted an underage chaplain out of the way. It was all very mysterious but I was only too glad to be free. It all seemed too good to be true, especially after I had decided that I had little to offer unbelieving soldiery. After the war I received the silver badge which disabled servicemen were given with the word *For Loyal Service*, so I can assume mine was an honourable discharge.

༄

A Mystery Solved

I have for many years had a conscience about my swift departure from the Army before the war was over. The Army is a harsh master which not only takes you over, body and soul, but does not relax its grip until an emergency comes to an end or until you are dead. As I previously wrote, my exit from the battle scene was less painful. A visit to wounded men of my regiment in Italy had resulted in a chance consultation with a friendly medical specialist and a period in hospital in Caserta about which I have remembered very little.

After finishing this book I dislodged from my bookshelf a recent book on the battle of Cassino by Matthew Parker which gave some space to shell-shocked men including Spike Milligan, late of the Goons. He and another had been admitted as 'bomb happy' to No. 2 General Hospital in Caserta because they had difficulty in walking and talking. They were treated by a psychiatrist, Major Harold Palmer, a tough no-nonsense northerner who used unorthodox methods to discover if they were really sick. To quote the book, 'a rugged-looking man with a broken nose who had written papers before the war about the value of narcosis for the treatment of phychiatric symptoms'. After being checked for malingering, a companion of Milligan's, called Salmon, remembered being given a drink and sent to bed. He then slept for two weeks and wakened to find he was cured of his symptoms by treatment known as deep sleep narcosis.

When I read this account I realised that I had been in the same hospital at that time and was given the same treatment. I remembered I had slept almost continuously for many days after having been interviewed by the same Major Palmer – who could forget the broken nose and rugged face? We were two soldiers who had been returned as unfit for frontline duties. I was given the alternative of a base chaplaincy in North Africa or a return home. I chose the latter and the Army decided I could not be used in further hostilities and would be discharged. Perhaps as I said earlier they had agreed with the medical specialist in Caserta that I was still too young to be in the Army at all.

Chapter Six

Aftermath of War – Naval Days

Here was I then, aged twenty-seven, unemployed, my wife shooting down doodlebugs at an anti-aircraft (AA battery) somewhere in England and I nobody's baby for my army life had put me outside any diocesan system. So far my priestly career had been decided for me, my first parish, an army career and my exit from it. What next? Meanwhile I was called to Cambridge to take charge of St Giles' Church where my first vicar had had a stroke. It was a wonderful return to the Catholic faith and practice with a young enthusiastic congregation. There I met Father Denis Marsh, a Francisan monk who suggested that I was the right man for Wellingborough School, as public school chaplain and senior Classics master. So off to Northhants I went to learn to be a teacher. I followed a well-known classical scholar, Henry Bettenson, who had translated *Documents Of The Early Church*. I was no scholar with little training in education. However my struggle with Latin and Greek at Cambridge made me understand the problems of my pupils and I was also able to take on a fifth-form English class. Much later in life I discovered I had a natural gift of empathy, an ability to enter the mind of others, invaluable for teachers.

Classroom teaching is exhausting, no easy option and coupled with doing locums in the holidays to earn extra money made me look for a change. It seemed that my period of training was ended and I was ready for that change. A short spell in a parish, three years in the Army among unbelieving fellow soldiers and now an apprenticeship in the teaching world, all with my faith unshaken, made me look for a challenge. Considering my military experience, I made what seems a strange choice. I allowed my name to go forward for a naval chaplaincy. Possibly the naval tradition in my mother's family influenced me or the unsettled state of parishes after the war. On the face of it the chance of being accepted seemed remote after my invaliding out of the Army. However the Chaplain of the Fleet did not discourage me and I was sent for a medical with a Surgeon Captain, Cyril May. I appeared healthy enough and he said, 'You have been playing rugger for the town side and have been teaching Classics; there's nothing wrong with you' and I was in. At a time when they were releasing wartime chaplains, I was taken on as Royal Naval Volunteer Reserve (RNVR) priest. It was a decision I have never regretted.

This decision enabled me to continue teaching. At a seminar in Cambridge I once heard a professor saying that the Navy had the best education system in Britain although it was not the most educated and this was born of necessity. Ships could only be safely entrusted at sea to professional sailors and this meant training them from scratch. In my day boys could be entered at $14\frac{1}{2}$, the school leaving age, and gradually prepared for the Fleet. I had three years at HMS *Ganges* on the east coast from 1951 where up to 1,800 were under training. Since many came from poor parts of the country with little education we had to provide basic teaching which included religious instruction. This kept the chaplains (three Anglicans) very busy especially since we offered Confirmation instruction. In my time we prepared a thousand candidates a year, with six Confirmation services each year. If this seems like a sausage machine, it should be said that they were all volunteers and enjoyed their course even though classes were held at 6.30 a.m. When they finished their training and went into the Fleet, they were recommended to seagoing chaplains. Many remained faithful and could provide a Christian nucleus in any ship.

Ganges provided me with a new experience. On Sunday mornings after Divisions all Anglican boys assembled in a covered part of the parade ground where a church had been rigged. The Royal Marine band provided the music for a shortened Mattins and sermon. Altogether there were nearly 2,000 in the congregation, including officers, and it was an art to preach to such a multitude and keep their attention. If the preacher was too long he was effectively 'given the bird' because a shuffling of feet on the hard concrete and sustained coughing made him inaudible. So the chaplains developed a short address which started with a story or illustration, then the moral or lesson, finally a short ending, in all, just over five minutes. As a result I have always found it difficult to preach much longer and I have held the record for short sermons in many parishes. Visiting preachers at *Ganges* who preached at length got the treatment and went away chastened men. Generally *Ganges* was great fun with plenty of sport and entertainment. One of my jobs was to organise the monthly dance for each division in turn. We had our Marine dance band and imported girls from nearby Ipswich in coaches. The challenge was to bring girls and boys together for they kept their distance at first but once brought together you could not keep them apart; they had to be prised apart for the return coach journey. This prompted the need for some sex instruction because it was clear that many of our boys knew little and would soon be turned loose in foreign ports where entertainment was more vicious. So the Captain decided that the chaplains would give sex education to all, an embarrassing task for the single priest! In the end it became impossible to fit it in with our other teaching commitments and a professional sex instructor was sent from the Home Office. It should be remembered that this was the 1950s in a less sex-ridden society. For my normal classes I introduced them to the Bible and used for this the Gideon New Testaments as text book. I was given several training establishments over the years, no doubt because of my school experience, and in all I was allotted teaching space.

Sandwiched between training was sea time, in those days

lengthy commissions. My first was for two years in the East
Indies. This gave time for a ship to develop as a family, chaplain included; a large family in the case of a cruiser or carrier.
    My first ship was HMS *Mauritius*, a Pompey-based cruiser.
Like most of the ships after the war she had already given
good service and needed modernisation. She had no air conditioning and this is was to prove a hardship in tropical climes.
I joined her in the spring of 1949 while she was still being
refitted and this not the best time to settle into one's new
home. Dockyard mateys were still at work, all services were
switched off and it was very dirty. For the necessities of
nature, I had to walk the ship's length, be saluted by the
officer of the watch before going ashore and use the 'heads'
(loo) beside the ship. Meals were taken in the barracks' wardroom. Anyway I had time to put my chapel on the bridge in
order and get to know some of my future shipmates.
    At last we were fit enough for the new commission to come
aboard. Officers lined the upper deck while the ship's
company was marched from the barracks: 800 men. As I
looked down upon my new parishioners I realised I had to
create a new church life from them and decided to try the
method I had used, albeit not very successfully, in the Army.
When all had settled into new quarters I started an early
morning Mass which was piped throughout the ship. A small
number came, more on Sunday and these formed a nucleus
from which I could work. It turned out very well and we
maintained a steady church life throughout the commission
despite difficult conditions.
    There are happy and unhappy ships in the Navy; which
would our commission be? Generally it has depended on the
captain. If he has authority, is respected and cares for all his
men he will probably have a happy ship. In fact he could learn
from St Benedict's *Rules for an Abbot* that he should be strict
with offenders but 'in administering correction he should act
prudently and not go to excess lest in seeking too eagerly to
scrape off the rust he brake the vessel'. On the first day after
commissioning the captain invited me to his cabin, I suppose
to see what he had been sent. He was short but well built with

a sea-worn red face, hair slightly greying and humorous eyes. On a shelf above his head I saw a copy of Bicknell's *Thirty-Nine Articles* and guessed he was going to be on my side. I was greeted in a most friendly way and asked what I would like to drink, it being about midday. Alcohol was still difficult to get just after the war and I chose whisky. 'You can't drink that before lunch,' he said and I quickly changed to pink gin. Ever since then I have never drunk whisky in the day nor offered it to anybody else. He was married to the daughter of a vicar and set a good example in his religious life. He was, in fact, a thoroughly good man and would have run a happy ship but for a small clique of officers who thought themselves above others and had dubious friends on shore. They were labelled 'social tits' and certainly made the most of hospitality in our ports of call. Of this there was plenty for the wardroom and entertainment could be exhausting; on one occasion we had to anchor downstream for twenty-four hours to recover from hospitality in the Persian Gulf. It seemed to me that the rest of the ship's company should not be forgotten and that they too should have a share in healthy entertainment ashore especially since some of the places we visited offered questionable 'delights'. So I followed the example of the chaplain of a former ship and encouraged families ashore to invite men into their homes. I was rarely disappointed and fixed up many with parties in places like Bombay, Karachi, Abadan in the Persian Gulf, Mauritius, Mombasa, Calcutta etc. The Navy has a term for being entertained ashore, 'strangling a baron' and after a while I found myself nicknamed 'Master Strangler'! It was very worthwhile and kept down cases of venereal disease during the commission.

All this took place over two years and meanwhile we had to do our working up because the cruiser had been laid up since the war. This was to be done off Malta and we set sail, stopping at Gilbraltar. Here I had an encounter which was to be repeated several times. I went with some junior officers to a nightclub where we met several friendly locals. Among these was Mr Randall who had served me in a duty-free shop. He was anxious to talk because he had drifted from the church over the years and wanted to return. As a result I was able to put him in contact with the Anglican procathedral. The Dean, Henry Lloyd, a former naval chaplain, took him under his wing and I heard years later he had become a valuable member of the congregation.

Next stop was Malta where we continued our working up exercises. It was four years after the war and the island was in a battered state and life was fairly primitive. Goats were milked on doorsteps, I remember, and of course there were no tourists. It was spring and the weather wonderful, blue skies and seas. From there we sailed through the Suez Canal to our base in Ceylon (now Sri Lanka) at Trincomalee, an excellent harbour surrounded by jungle. From here we sailed to cover much of Southeast Asia.

When we left Aden we entered a world mostly forgotten in the twenty-first century. Despite a shake-up in the Second World War this world apart from India, was still awaiting development and undiscovered by tourists chiefly because general air travel was still in an early stage. Almost immediately after arrival on station we were sent up the Persian Gulf to bring back the crews of frigates we had handed over to the Persians and we sailed into extreme heat – it was July 1949. We could see little signs of industrial activity along the shore of the Gulf, only Arab villages, until we reached the northern part. Then the smell of oil filled the air and we went alongside the quay of the Anglo-Iranian Oil company which was then in British hands. Here the heat was so dreadful that it was said you could fry an egg on the upper deck. Ashore there was air conditioning, but as I have said before, there was none on board our ship and we sailed away as quickly as possible. Later in the year in the winter months we returned to Abadan and were given a right royal reception by the British and Americans who worked there and were glad to see new faces. Lavish entertainment was organised along with sporting activities of many kinds. On the way up we anchored off Bahrein where there was a growing British community which was the forerunner of a future massive oil industry. We gave a cocktail party and since we were a little distance from the shore guests had to be brought by our boats. The Royal Marine band was playing and drinks were being served when without warning a *shamal* or violent storm blew up which stirred huge waves and made it impossible for anybody to leave. This caused great alarm for young couples who had left children ashore. But nothing could be done and we had to accommodate guests on board. Cabins were given up and some slept in hammocks to the surprise of the duty ratings the next morning who gave the usual 'wakey-wakey!' By morning the sea had suddenly subsided and people could leave – was this the kind of storm which had blown up many years before when Jesus and his disciples were caught in a sudden storm on the Sea of Galilee? I was left ashore to baptise and give Anglicans a Eucharist and spent the night in palatial quarters built for future oil presidents. The local sheikh entertained some of the officers to an evening meal when we sat round the roast carcasses of several sheep.

The next morning I was flown in an ancient aircraft to join the ship at Kuwait, where an advance party of oil technicians lived in wooden huts. Many years later my flight stopped at Dubai and I could scarcely believe the transformation into high-rise buildings and modern civilisation which had taken place. On our return journey we stopped at Musqat to pay our respects to the local sheikh who lived simply in a small village. Only eight Europeans lived there and I was lucky enough to be invited to a curry lunch and endless gin by the English doctor.

Later we visited East Africa and went alongside at the Seychelles which were still isolated from the world with only a visit from a ship every three months. I was warned that a large percentage of women were diseased and had to be kept from our sailors, which was difficult because they were very attractive. A dance was organised and a brew of Empire port-type wine flowed. I took a regulating petty officer with a squad of men and we quietly removed any drunks and sent them back to the ship. The result was that we had very few 'casualties'. The duties of a chaplain were manifold!

Since I was also sports and entertainment officer I was kept very busy in the ports we visited because local teams were very anxious to play against us and win. I was also expected to preach ashore and this meant adapting to different congregations, Sinhalese, Malayans, Africans, Indian and so on. We organised a full church parade in Karachi and afterwards the ratings were invited to the gymkhana clubhouse for alcoholic refreshments. The officers returned to the ship to entertain VIPs to drinks on the quarterdeck. We were in the middle of this when lorries screeched up the quay and sailors were helped or carried noisily on board. A lady guest asked me where they had been to which I had to reply, 'To church'!

We had a two months' refit in Singapore dockyard and lived ashore in what were still simple Chinese surroundings, recovering from the devastating Japanese occupation. There was jungle warfare with Chinese Communists and I went with the Royal Marines to reinforce British forces.

As I have said life east of Aden had changed little since colonial days. India was the exception. A year before we arrived Mountbatten had managed with some bloodshed to divide the continent into India and Pakistan. Our job was to assist both the Royal Indian Navy and the Royal Pakistan Navy so we exercised with both at sea and visited both Indian and Pakistani ports. Bombay had become a 'dry' area as far as alcohol was concerned and we could only entertain the locals to tea and cakes. To continue to drink meant applying for an alcoholic's licence. The Indian Navy was not happy about this and an Instructor, Commander Setna, organised licences for us. Since people ashore managed to entertain us with private supplies we did not have to use our licences which were collected by Setna just before we sailed, no doubt for supplying his own officers. This was the only time in my life I have been declared a certified alcoholic!

The highlight of our commission was being able to spend weeks in Newara Eliya, the hill country of Ceylon. Here was a rest camp during the war. HMS *Uva* was built at Diyatalawa where the air was cool and bracing compared with the sweaty heat round the coast. While the ship was having a minor refit – bottom scraped – in Colombo dockyard, the ship's company were sent up in two watches to this beautiful place, among the tea plantations. As sports officer and chaplain I looked after both watches so had six weeks there altogether. There were many young British planters there who were keen to play rugger, hockey and cricket against us. Buried in the thick undergrowth was a church which had been built for our men in the war and then forgotten. With some help I uncovered it and discovered that it was well-equipped inside. I remember finding a chest full of Mass vestments but saw they were moving. A family of huge cockroaches had occupied them and had to be emptied on to the compound outside the vestry. They fell helplessly on their backs and were efficiently dismembered by tribes of ants nearby. It was Easter time and I was able to advertise a programme of services. When I arrived for early Mass I saw a long procession of local Christians, Anglicans in beautiful clothes, winding up the hill, a sight I shall long remember. There were so many that there was scarcely room for my own men. Our Church was truly alive on that island!

This is not meant to be a travelogue but I have taken up space because it was another stage of my development. Not only did it broaden my experience of the Church overseas, it gave me a further authority. The Navy, unlike the Army, treats its chaplains well and gives them the status of head of a department in a ship which gives them a voice when important decisions are made. To some extent this depends on the captain. This happened in my first sea commission. As I have said I enjoyed the support of my first captain but halfway through the commission he returned home and was replaced by one not so friendly who was of uncertain temperament. First thing in the morning his steward would look into his cabin, then report either 'Bright and breezy' or 'Lousy keep out', an uncertainty which did not make for the happiness of the ship. Fortunately my position as sports officer carried some weight. A naval chaplain has no rank and this enables him to be on equal terms with both fellow officers and also with ratings. Captains anxious for promotion take care to remain on good terms with their chaplains!

All this gave me some confidence for my next sea commission three years later. In the spring of 1954 I was appointed to HMS *Glasgow*, another Pompey cruiser and flagship of the Commander in Chief in the Mediterranean, Admiral Mountbatten. He had the reputation of not suffering fools gladly but I found him easy to get on with, possibly because we shared a Cambridge college, Christ's, where he studied after the First World War. Like most sailors he was happiest when at sea and merged easily into the ship's life. His secretary, Ronnie Brockman, was a good churchman and was a regular communicant when on board. The presence of the Admiral's staff meant that my chapel had to be turned into quarters for them and I was pushed out. However the chippies made me a wooden portable altar (which I still use) so that I could set up shop wherever I could find a space – rather like my Army days! One evening when we were having our drinks before dinner, the Admiral came into the wardroom and said, 'Padre, they are asking questions about you in Parliament.' This was a surprise because I had made no complaint but it seemed that some devout rating had written home about the absence of a chapel and this had made its way, via an MP, to the House. At once there was a flurry of activity to remedy the problem and I found myself with a very adequate chapel in the starboard waist.* Dickie Mountbatten had acted very quickly! When we were at sea on Sundays and the admiral's family was in company in a frigate, I was transferred at sea over the waves clutching my church box so that I could take a service for Edwina and Pamela. You don't get better than that!

In fact, Lady Mountbatten worked closely with me when I chartered a plane to bring sailors' families out to Malta while our ship was being refitted and made certain that there was an adequate supply of blankets and sheets for them and generally made certain they had a good time. On several occasions I was included in a Mountbatten party when they visited interesting places ashore, such as Roman ruins in North Africa.

---

* The middle part of the ship.

Glasgow was on a General Service Commission, an innovation which cut down the time ships spent overseas. This meant we had a year abroad and six months in the Home Fleet. So we left the Mediterranean and returned to Portsmouth, resigned to having a dull time doing Navy Days round our coasts. In the autumn of 1955 we were anchored off the pier at the unromantic resort of Southend-on-Sea, and were giving the usual cocktail party for the locals when a number of reporters were ferried out to us and housed in cabins. We then learnt that we were bound for an interesting destination, finally revealed as Poland. We were to be the first ship after the war to go behind the Iron Curtain. So we sailed across the North Sea through the Skaggerak into the Baltic and so to the port of Gdynia. Here a Polish guard of honour was drawn up and a discordant sound ascended which proved to be our national anthem. It was now the turn of our captain to pay his respects. I should have said that our captain for the whole commission was Peter Dawnay who was married to the sister of the Duchess of Gloucester and this almost 'royal' was driven away to the Communist headquarters to meet the local commissar, an interesting encounter! All seemed to go well and the officials were called 'decent types'. Poland at that time was in the firm grip of Russia and was at near starvation point. Meanwhile, a liaison officer came aboard to arrange some entertainment. I found myself arranging a football match between our team and a local side on the barracks sports ground. Officers were invited to a reception that evening at the local HQ which promised to be a bleak affair in view of the cheerless conditions. So we left instructions for our dinners to be kept and a large party of officers and press reporters were driven off through streets full of queues of locals outside empty shops. There was a different picture inside a hall where many officials with their wives were waiting to greet us. Tables groaned under the weight of dishes of delicacies, such as smoked salmon, golden and black caviar and bottles of good Georgian wine and vodka. In no time at all a jolly party began and we were all friends. I think it was one of the most sumptuous meals I have ever had and I noticed the local officials and their families making the most of the spread. I could not help remembering the hungry Poles outside. We had been warned before we left the ship of the dangers of too much vodka and the wardroom acquitted itself well but the press men did not and had to be lifted back on board where they were very sick indeed.

Then there was the soccer match. We had one of the worst teams in the Fleet but looked forward to a friendly game. Imagine our surprise when our coach drove us past the barracks on to a large stadium full of people. I watched as a very professional Polish side trotted on to the field followed by our men in their faded ship's strip. It soon became clear that we were very badly matched as the Poles knocked in goal after goal. The crowd began to laugh for they realised what had happened; the Brits were to be shown up. After ten goals a voice came over the tannoy and a friendly Pole beside me laughed. 'It says "That's enough, Polish team",' he said and for the rest of the game despite many chances, no more goals were scored.

The visit ended happily with a wonderful Russian song and dance show and we sailed back home to a different political scene, having first to remove a few stowaways who had hidden themselves in corners of the ship, helped, I suspect, by some of our ship's company who had been heartbroken by conditions ashore.

Glasgow paid off in the autumn and we all went to other ships. I had a short spell in a training establishment in Yorkshire, and then had nearly three years ashore in Malta. It was a very crowded commission because I had not only a parish life on Manoel Island but destroyers and frigates to look after and teaching at the naval school at Tal Handak. This was a comprehensive school for service children; 2000 in my day. I also did some coaching in Latin and English.

There was also much welfare work to be done among naval families. Some wives did not settle easily abroad, despite the lovely hot weather, and pined for life at home. In later years the three services developed an efficient welfare department but for most of my time, problems came to the chaplains helped sometimes by petty officer Wrens.

I had a number of problems with families in Malta but none

so strange as one involving a childless couple, an unwanted baby and a prostitutes' ring. It all started when an able seaman and his wife came to my office to ask how they could adopt a child, preferably a boy. They had seen that Maltese women gave birth to a number of children and hoped they could adopt one. I said this was impossible on a Roman Catholic island and they went away disappointed. By chance I met a young telegraphist who had been with me at *Ganges*. He was married and had his wife with him on the island. She had just given birth again and found it difficult to manage two children in the heat. She was threatening to return home to her mother. Did I know anybody willing to take the baby? I immediately thought of my able seaman Shave and his wife Betty and suggested a transfer. They were delighted and with the help of a petty officer welfare Wren I took charge of the child which was very badly cared for and handed it over. Fortunately it was a boy and Betty was delighted. From then on I became their favourite man and was always welcomed to their house. So I was able to keep an eye on the child who was being over-whelmed with care and attention.

This was not the end of the affair. At that time naval author-ities were concerned because a company of Royal Marines who were training on the island were using a prostitute ring for their comforts. I was asked to help. Some time later I met the young telegraphist whom I had helped with the baby. He came to my office and I noticed he had been badly knocked about and had a black eye. I slowly extracted the story from him. It seemed that relieved of one child his wife had 'gone on the game' and with other naval wives pleasured lonely Royal Marines. She promised her husband she would buy him a motorbike with some of the money she earned provided he kept out of the way at certain times. Unfortunately he had returned too soon and disturbed a marine *in mediis rebus*, to quote the Latin for 'full flow', and was beaten up. I was able to pass on this information; the ring was broken up and the naval families sent home, including my young telegraphist friend whom I never saw again.

All was quiet on the Maltese front until the time came for the

Shaves to return home with the child. He had never been properly adopted because Maltese law did not allow adoptions for couples under fifty. So how could we get them off the island? It all seemed very difficult until I sought help from a Maltese friend, George Zarb. He managed Malta Airlines and in a former commission I had chartered a plane from him, in the face of keen competition, for bringing families out from England when our ship was refitting. He had a friend in the government who might fix it. So we met this official over lunch and after a full flow of wine became such good friends that he promised he would sign the necessary form for getting the child off the island. So the Shaves went home and the last I heard of them was a Christmas card which said they had retired and were settled in Cornwall. Just part of a padre's job!

After my family and I left the island Mintoff led his campaign for independence; the British were pushed out and gradually the Navy disappeared from its base and Malta became the prey of tourists.

Back in England I was appointed to HMS *Seahawk*, Culdrose, on the Lizard, a growing air station which was changing from fixed-wing aircraft to helicopters. This was my first experience of the air world which had developed a lifestyle of its own. Pilots tended to live on their nerves and ground crews were better paid than other ratings. This posed considerable welfare problems and extra work for chaplains. Cornwall is a beautiful and romantic part of Britain which through history has developed its own way of life. When you cross the Tamar you leave England and the sophistications of city life for another land. Naval wives had to adapt to a quieter way of life and some did not; no Bingo halls and fine cinemas and a long distance from parents and other relatives. It did not help that extra pay meant hard drinking and family rows. Although some officers and men had married quarters, others did not and had to find accommodation anywhere possible in surrounding villages. I was repeatedly called out to settle welfare problems. I remember having to drive through pouring rain to a house on the Lizard where the husband had returned drunk the night before and beaten up his wife. As evidence she pointed to a vivid orange patch on the wall, the remains of a plate of tomato soup hurled by her husband.

It did not help that we had a large unit of Wrens on the station working close to the men and these could be a daily temptation. I remember being asked by a 'schoolie' divisional officer to find out what was troubling one of his best petty officers. After a gentle probing I learnt that his wife was accusing him of having an affair with a Wren. She accused him of making love on the beach and then bringing the girl back to his married quarters. I then visited the wife who was insistent that the facts were true. 'It was after I had gone to bed,' she said, 'and I heard them downstairs. The next morning I found sand on the sitting room carpet.' The petty officer denied all this and insisted that he had never had a relationship with anybody else. He had merely worked beside a Wren in the Met. Office. The wife then produced as evidence her parents who had come from their home in Warrington near Manchester and said they had hidden outside the house and watched the husband and girl go into the house. Neither side budged and the man became ill with worry. Then suddenly the scene changed. I went to the home and found it closed up and silent. A neighbour said the wife had suddenly packed up her belongings and gone back to Warrington. In the end we discovered that she hated Cornwall and wanted to go to her parents. Her story had been a pack of lies to get herself out of something she did not like.

On top of this I had an excellent church life on the station with a family Mass on Sundays and good congregations. But I was given no rest from welfare cases by day or night and the visiting bishop to the Forces, Stanley Betts, was concerned and handed me over to the doctors who diagnosed a skin condition caused by too much pressure and I was recommended for invalidity from the Navy. Both the Chaplain of the Fleet, John Armstrong, and the Second Sea Lord tried to prevent this but the medics had the last word and I found myself in Stonehouse Naval Hospital awaiting discharge and within a short time I went on the retired RN list.

PART TWO

Chapter Seven

Another World

Once again I found myself in the outside world. For eighteen years my life had been organised by the Royal Navy (apart from three in the Army under war conditions) and now I had to fend for myself in a different environment. I can now, from a distance, understand the contrast between the two ways of life, the one with very high standards of conduct and efficiency, the other where standards were rapidly declining in work and daily life. Once the monarch and their Lordships of the Admiralty were assured of the character and ability of an entrant they granted a commission to observe and execute King's (this was in the 1940s) Regulations and Admiralty Instructions ... and chaplains were under the same orders. Only death or their Lordships' pleasure could release from that obligation.

In fact there was a similarity between this commitment and the monastic life. Just as a novice had to promise obedience, stability and change of lifestyle so a naval officer had to obey orders, settle down in a new way of life and transform his life into one of service. It was a wonderful way of life for those who could fit into a mould fashioned by generations of seafaring men. 'Forsaking all others' would be a suitable description of what was required and this of course has applied particularly to those who enter a Benedictine community. So a naval officer had to be adaptable and sociable, clubbable because he has to fit into any collection of fellow officers in the same ship. A ship's safety demands a high standard of efficiency and attention to detail and its reputation relies on the way officers dress and conduct themselves in public.

In exchange for such a surrender of personal liberty the Navy throws a protective shield round its members and has its own administration and its own morality. Is not Horatio Nelson its patron saint? Not without reason is the toast drunk at dinner on Saturdays at sea, 'To sweethearts and wives, may they never meet!' It also has its own language fashioned by centuries of life at sea.

All this I left behind me as I stumbled into the outside world where standards were lower in many ways, especially in dress and reliability. As the Navy's numbers increasingly dwindle I regret the decline of the Navy pensioner who in civilian life can be entrusted with difficult jobs. To tell the truth I was not too sorry to leave a way of life which was becoming less satisfying with shorter commissions and increasing economies.

So where could I turn? As far as the official Church was concerned I was nobody's baby for I had conducted my priest's life adrift from any special diocesan loyalty. I had been able to move easily between church life and outside duties, something which has always suited me well. In fact, I need not have worried for news went round ecclesiastical circles that I was available and several attractive offers were put before me. My old college friend David Say, now Bishop of Rochester, offered two large parishes and this was kind because we differed in churchmanship. However, I felt I needed time to settle down again in a Church which was being forced to bring itself into the modern world. So I accepted the small country living of Lanteglos-by-Fowey in Cornwall. This was basically a fishing village with three churches, one in Polruan, one a beautiful Early English church, a mile and a half beside a farm and a small building looked after by Angela du Maurier, the sister of Daphne. It was a romantic part of the coast used by Daphne in some of her novels. In 1962 the parish still belonged mostly to the locals although retired people were beginning to settle there until they found the steep hills too much for them. Most of the population were in Polruan where a church had been built in 1900 and had been looked after by a famous Anglo-Catholic priest, Father Bernard Walke. He went on to St Hilary which he made a cultural centre until he was driven out by a Protestant bishop of Truro and finally went to Rome. He laid a strong Catholic foundation at Polruan which survived less Catholic practice by later vicars and could easily be revived. It is said that Catholic pioneers in Cornwall were soon forgotten but I found that where the faith had been well taught it was never lost and this was true of my new parish. I started a children's Mass on Saturdays and a youth club in the week and congregations grew, which did not please a small, old brigade of single women who promptly left and never came to church again. This 'oldies versus change' was not unusual as I found later round the country.

While still in the Navy I had become friendly with the very Catholic vicar of St Mary's Penzance, Arthur Williams who then became Archdeacon of Bodmin. He not only found money to refurbish my vicarage but used me to prod Catholic societies and the Federation of Catholic Priests into action. There was a rising concern at moves to bring Anglicans and Methodists together and Cornishmen knew it would not work in their diocese. So I became secretary of the local Church Union and visited many parishes and got an informed debate going which later bore fruit when an actual scheme for Anglican/Methodist reunion was put before the Church Assembly for a vote but that is another story. Meanwhile I was elected to the Church Union councils in London.

I enjoyed my time at Polruan and found time for reading. The Second Vatican Council was about to meet in Rome under John XXIII and it was rumoured that an *aggionarmento*, or renewal, was in the air. It was fortunate that I gave myself a course on possible changes in the liturgy in view of what was to happen. Dom Gregory Dix's book *The Shape of the Liturgy* published in 1943, had roused my interest because it was clear that many of us found the restrictions of the Book of Common Prayer Communion Service out of date. The Roman Catholic

Church on the Continent was crying out for the Mass to be brought nearer to the people and a Jesuit priest Joseph Jungmann was providing necessary scholarship. I read his great work, *Solemnia Missae, The Mass of the Roman Rite* and was excited by it despite its considerable detail. Other writers were also crying out for change in several areas of church life but few, I think, were prepared for the radical measures set out in Vatican Council encyclical, which poured out in a constant stream over the next few years. It also became clear that such change would in time affect the Anglican Church and so it happened. So in a way I equipped myself to understand and teach what was happening while I was still beside the still waters of Cornwall.

As a retired naval chaplain I might have remained in my country parish for ever but one day in 1966 I received a phone call from Church Union Headquarters asking me if I would take on the job of organising secretary in London. It was a call I could not resist so my family and I packed our bags and set out to find a house near my office in west London. I was lucky for a rector in Surrey offered me a house for duty in Blechingley.

Chapter Eight

Another Kind of Command

I had been a member of the Church Union for some years, as were my parents and even my grandfather so my family had a connection with its beginning in the middle of the nineteenth century. But most of my friends did not know what the Church Union was and this was a foretaste of what my first work would be. Many thought it was something to do with politics, a union of churchmen, perhaps to get more power or even money and in some respects they were right. In 1833 some priests in Oxford began a campaign to bring back Catholic faith and practice into the Church of England. This was not generally popular with the nation and fierce Protestants tried by different means to prevent the spread of this new movement. Priests were attacked by mobs as they tried to carry out their priestly duties. Queen Victoria was not amused nor were some members of Parliament. There was a move to bring in legislation to remove from the Book of Common Prayer any references to our Catholic heritage. So in order to protect priests who were being persecuted by Protestants a society of chiefly lay people called the English Church Union was founded in 1860 and this set about fighting opposition. It could not prevent the sending to prison of several priests who refused to give up what we today would call moderate ritual practices but Protestants' aggression was blunted and the Catholic movement went from strength to strength until it emerged triumphant between the war years, supported by the Church Union. A series of Anglo-Catholic congresses were held in the Albert Hall. These were cut short by the Second World War and afterwards for several reasons the Church Union began to fade, possibly because the Catholic cause seemed to have won. Branches round the country which had been the strength of the Union became weak and importance was found in its theological and publishing work. In the 1950s another congress could raise some support and this made a contribution to the liturgical debate which was beginning. I therefore entered the scene in 1966 when interest had waned but one final congress was planned. My first job was to go the the South Bank and sign a contract to take over the Royal Festival Hall for four days in April 1968. A committee had been formed to organise this but as the months went by they often proved a hindrance rather than a help and in the end I was left to do most of the work. In fact I also found the Union's executive committee which made all decisions to be very difficult to work with. It comprised priests and laymen, some of whom had held office far too long and were dyed in the wool old-fashioned Catholics. My colleague was Father F. C. (Percy) Coleman who dealt with general and theological matters. Although a fundamentally nice man he appeared condescending and distant which did not help with ordinary parish members. He gave the impression that he thought me an ignorant naval officer but fortunately gave me a free hand in my work round the country. His successor, Fr Douglas Carter, was even more withdrawn and in time I found I was saddled with more and more other work, pilgrimage, publishing and charitable trusts. Luckily I had a good secretary, Kate Rogers, middle-aged and capable, who kept an eagle eye on my desk work.

Clearly my first task was to increase membership round the country and this meant a lot of travelling. I saw parts of Britain I had never seen before and slept in a variety of beds in vicarages where I was treated with different hospitality. It became possible to make a star-rating list. Some clergy wives treated me with near reverence and would not presume to eat at the same table; to others I was an extra nuisance as they wrestled with ill-disciplined children. There were other hazards. I remember going to Blackpool to talk to priests there and being housed for the night in the vicarage on the cliffs. It was the season of the Illuminations and a large pink elephant, decorated with flashing lights, disturbed my sleep that night. On another occasion I had to go by rail to Rotherham without time for lunch. Due to a bad connection, I arrived late for an afternoon meeting of the Mothers' Union. 'No time for food, I'm afraid,' said the young vicar, 'but drink this for the time being,' and he thrust a tumbler of brown liquid at me. I gulped it down only to realise it was neat whisky! Thus inspired I delivered my message to a church full of women, taking good care nobody smelt my breath. Then there was the meeting of students in the beer cellar of Durham University, this time with a tankard of beer in my hand – a pleasant occasion. A brief visit to the Isle of Man, another to the Isle of Wight, then Jersey, to Walsingham, to the slums of Nottingham, then the contrast of the posh part of Taunton, made up an increasingly busy schedule. The size of my audiences varied considerably and I found by listening to the reading of the minutes of the last meeting that little attempt had been made to come to grips with the mounting religious issues of the day. The Second Vatican Council continued to pour out encyclicals on matters of Catholic faith, some like the changes in the Mass affected the laity who were confused because their local clergy did not explain them. The Anglican Church responded by issuing two revised orders of the Eucharist, Series One which kept the old Prayer Book language but changed the order and Series Two which changed both. Some priests, excited by the similarity to the new Roman rites but without training in liturgiology also imposed them on their people without explanation.

I had a personal experience of this confusion. I was asked to do a locum at a church in Jersey. I arrived on the feast of Corpus Christi just as the vicar was leaving for the mainland, saying I was booked to sing Mass that evening. 'What rite?' I shouted at his departing figure. 'Series Two,' he shouted back. Came the evening and I confidently began the service.

After a time I felt that neither the organist not the congregation were with me but we somehow soldiered on and at least
ended together. I then discovered they had never had Series
Two before but I had been made the guinea pig to introduce
it. So for the rest of my stay which was very pleasant I gave
them a short course on the Eucharist and what the changes
meant.

This was only one of several experiences. Often I found that
branch meetings were used to give entertaining, sometimes
almost frivolous talks, scarcely involving the Church, like
'Birds I have seen in the local churchyard'! Poor souls,
they had been given little guidance from Union central
office about important agendas and this was an urgent
matter. Changes in the Mass were obviously worrying
people and priests seemed unable to reassure them. Just as
some Roman Catholics stopped going to Mass because the
old Latin rite was disappearing, so some Anglicans lapsed
because the 'dear old Book of Common Prayer was not
being used at Communion'. It was clear something had to
be done and here I blessed the time I had spent in Cornwall
studying liturgy. I now began to use meetings to give talks
on 'What is Happening to our Service?'. One talk was put
on tape and my secretary said it could be turned into a
booklet. So the first of what was called the *What's Happening* series was published and proved popular; many thousands were printed at a small cost. The ignorant sailor
began to show his literary teeth!

The *aggiornamento* in Rome brought wider changes, not
least in disciplines. The fast before Communion was shortened and evening Masses became popular. Generally Christians became Easter rather than Good Friday people.
Mediaeval theology stressed gaining salvation through
penance and grace, entering into the sufferings of Christ
with forty joyful days of Eastertide as a kind of adjunct and
the Book of Common Prayer followed suit at the Reformation. For instance for most of the year in the Anglican
liturgy the only mention of the resurrection of Jesus was
found in a few words in the Creed and the Holy Commu-

nion service was described as instituted just for the remembrance of Christ's death – no more. Now Easter became the central theme throughout the Church's year and union with the risen and glorified Lord became the inspiration of the devout Christian. I wrote another booklet called *Easter Everyday* which explained the change in spirituality but balanced it with another, *What's Happening to our Discipline* in which I described the duties which were still essential if we wanted to stay in the risen Lord's company. This was not generally realised.

Meanwhile preparations were continuing for our Congress in 1968 for which we gave the title 'All Things New' which perhaps was not strictly true. I employed a cousin, Carol Jeffries, an art student, to do the design with a paschal candle as the main emblem. In my book, *Marginal Catholics*, I have given a sketch of what happened. As far as numbers were concerned it was a success. We had four thousand at the first Mass in the Festival Hall which used the new Series One order and was concelebrated by five bishops and two priests. The MC and servers were experienced hands and ensured there were no slip-ups. I used seventy assisting priests to give Communion and finished in an hour, just in time to greet Princess Margaret who came to the reception afterwards. Our speakers, led by Archbishop Michael Ramsey spoke well and people went away with new enthusiasm. The congress had certainly given the Church Union a new life and my next job was to plan for the future. I edited the account of the congress with all the speeches and am able to look back at them.

In the light of the near forty years which followed I can see they did not attempt to deal with what became a pressing subject, New Testament theology. I shall be dealing with this later in my book but will mention here the history of radical ideas about the Gospels. For two hundred years German and then English scholars had increasingly raised doubts whether the Gospels were eyewitness and reliable accounts of our Lord's ministry on earth and he was steadily being reduced to a mere moral teacher deprived of his divinity. I remember about this time a leading Anglo-Catholic priest saying to me that we had made the mistake of concentrating between the wars on worship and not taking note of what was happening in liberal biblical theology. We were still neglecting these studies in the 1960s and were content to allow reputedly Catholic scholars like Nineham and Houlden to manage that side of things on behalf of the rest of the Catholic movement. As I hope to show it was a deadly mistake from which we are still slowly recovering today.

Meanwhile another crisis was upon us because the scheme for the reunion of Anglicans and Methodists was due to come before the Church assembly in 1969. A chapter in *Marginal Catholics* on what followed has been called the fullest account of the affair. My four years in Cornwall and my subsequent journeys round the country had convinced me that neither church was ready for this at this time.

Chapter Nine

Towards the Wilderness

It has been said that if you scratch an Englishman you will find a fear of Rome under the skin. Through the influence of the good Pope John Paul this fear has somewhat abated and yet there remains the idea that Roman Catholics are different and not fully integrated into our national life. No doubt a reason for a continuing fear could be found embedded in history. After the Reformation there were attempts by foreign powers to invade Britain and bring her back to the true Catholic faith and thereafter there was a kind of running battle between Catholics and Protestants to seize the upper hand in politics. The first Tractarians therefore faced an uphill struggle as they showed that the Church of England had retained a Catholic inheritance and sought to implement it both in faith and practice. A cry of disloyalty was aimed at them and Queen Victoria did not disguise her distaste for these Ritualists. 'The defiance shown by the Clergy of the High Church and Ritualistic party is so great that something must be done to check it and prevent its continuing,' she wrote in a private letter to the Archbishop of Canterbury. But attempts failed and the movement went from strength to strength. I was born into the greater years of this Catholic movement and have always believed that I was a simply a Catholic separated from the main part of the Roman Catholic Church by an accident. This has carried me through many a crisis of identity and is helpful in the present twenty-first century when the Church of England has gone astray. I know I am not quite kosher and only a marginal Catholic as I explained in an earlier book of that name, but it has carried me through until the present day.

So I was on a periphery between the main Church and outer darkness, or wilderness, and although I did not realise it I was about to be forced into the latter. For it seemed that the Anglican Establishment had set its heart on being ecumenical and was committed to doing something about the Methodist Church from which it had been long separated. This getting together again was clearly going to be a messy business because the Methodists and Wesleyans had taken on board some very un-Anglican habits after they had gone their own way some two centuries before. However representatives from both churches met to find out if there was any mileage in planning a reconciliation. Both sides had their different theological views representing high, low and middle of the way and almost all were academics. Anglican Catholic opinion rested with Fr Harold Riley who had been secretary of the Church Union. Dr Eric Kemp, a Fellow of Exeter College, Oxford who was one of the chief architects of the final scheme but later became a champion of the Catholic cause in future controversies but had not yet shown his hand. Official conversations had begun in 1956 and enough progress was made for a report to be published in 1963. Agreement had been made easier by the withdrawal of Methodist dissentients. Since Fr Riley seemed to be happy with the proposals, Catholics rested happily. This was roughly the position when I entered the scene in 1966 as organising secretary. Although the scheme of reunion hung over us at that time there was little urgency to make decisions and anyway we were preparing for our Congress. When this was over we found serious proposals for reunion were being put before us and urgent Church Union meetings were arranged round the country which I had to address. I was under no illusions about obstacles for reunion because I had lived and worked among Methodists in Cornwall where division was still strong. I remember my lady organist in Polruan brought some clothing for our autumn fair.

'I hope they are all right', said my wife dubiously. 'Oh yes,' replied the other, 'Church not Chapel!' This perhaps sums up the religious atmosphere in a small community and I had found Methodists difficult to deal with. They were worthy but perhaps too worthy possibly because they did not share all the pleasures of other people, like drinking. Their ideal of holiness seemed to have rubbed off on them without penetrating too far below the surface.

Anyway, we seemed to be on course for some sort of reunion so I left my efforts to commend Vatican II to our members and turned to studying what was proposed. It appeared to centre on a Service of Reconciliation when clergy from both sides would come together round the country and there would be a mutual laying on of hands, thereby uniting ministries. Since bishops would act on behalf of Anglicans it could be said that Methodist clergy would be episcopally ordained, something they were unwilling to accept. So less definite wording was used at the Service of Reconciliation: 'Each prayed that God would give to the other the distinctive characteristics which it believed it had received from Him.' This meant little to Anglican priests who believed that their ministry was already complete. Before this service there would be an increasing cooperation between two distinctive churches until final union was possible.

The reports on the progress of the conversations between the two sets of representatives of course went into greater detail, nevertheless the end result was to be the Service of Reconciliation and the joining together of the two churches. So having studied the different documents critically, I saw there were a number of snags from the Anglican-Catholic point of view. First of all, doubts were raised as to whether the Service of Reconciliation could be a traditional episcopal ordination, especially since the Methodists did not want it. The Old Catholic Church in Europe who were in Communion with the Anglican Church gave a thumbs down when consulted and said it would destroy future relationships.

There were other concerns. The Methodist Church had close contacts with other Free Churches and was unwilling to end this relationship. This meant that Anglicans could become involved with very unlikely bedfellows and there would be a complete breakdown of orthodoxy. Then, there were Methodist women ministers, some in top positions, and they would introduce into the reunited churches the prospect of women priests which at that time the Anglican Church could not contemplate. There was also lay celebration of Holy Communion in some Methodist areas of the country and in some cases baptism was not even essential. There were other anomalies such as non-alcoholic wine and marriage discipline. All these objections seemed unsurmountable for an Anglican and it is difficult to understand how Fr Riley, a prominent Anglo-Catholic, could have given a seal of approval to the final scheme. Yet even Michael Ramsey who was regarded as a Catholic Archbishop of Canterbury and the main speaker at out recent Church Congress was known to be in favour as was, and more awkwardly still, my colleague Fr Coleman. It seemed the odds were being stacked against us and unless we could provide strong opposition we were in a thoroughly unacceptable situation. Most of the diocesan bishops were prepared to vote for the scheme except one or two and the Bishop of Willesden, Graham Leonard, a real Athanasius *contra mundum* who headed the opposition. Anybody who dared oppose the main body of the Establishment was not going to be popular, but I knew the scheme was unworkable and was prepared to say so. I have written a full account of the Anglican/Methodist affair in *Marginal Catholics* and would hesitate to write more about it but for the fact that more than thirty years later conversations between the two churches have been resumed and in these days of more liberal Anglican theology are more likely to succeed. In fact I note little change in the differences of faith and practice which I saw and heard as I moved round the country in 1969. So I had first to explain to Church Union branches what was being proposed by architects of the reunion scheme and here I faced a difficulty because there was a lack of sound Catholic teaching, even in some of our foremost parishes. Whereas in the early days of the Catholic revival most laity knew what they were fighting for, basic doctrinal teaching had now been lost in liturgical success. In other words parishes could have full Catholic worship and practice without learning what lay behind them. Words like 'apostolic succession' and 'valid sacraments' meant little to happy worshippers and I had the job of starting from the beginning before moving on to matters of the moment, which were of course the rights and wrongs of the present reunion proposals. As I addressed Methodist audiences, I found they, too, were short of basic teaching.

Both sides were happy with St Paul's description in 1 Corinthians 9:24–27, of playing games to win the prize of heaven but were employing different rules. Perhaps Anglicans were using Rugby Union rules while Methodists were playing soccer! To throw them both into the arena without agreement would end in confusion. If one side refused to change the game could not begin. As I have said there were several Methodist practices which they were not willing to give up. I lived for eight years in a 'gin and jag' parish while I was running the Church Union and helped at the local church where the main Sunday service was Sung Eucharist. On Sunday evening we had a interchange with the local chapel, one week the Methodists joined our sung evensong and the next week we went to their worship which was a hymn sandwich centred round a long sermon which I felt they enjoyed as one might enjoy a good meal. Instead of saints' days they had their anniversaries which might have a Communion service tacked on. There was no sense of priesthood and in some areas I visited there was lay celebration and an almost Puritan lifestyle. To balance this there was a 'High Church' form of Methodist churchmanship where there was little to choose outwardly between a moderate Anglican vicar and the local minister. For instance I was asked to join a debate in Canterbury with a local vicar, the local minister and a Voice of Methodism speaker who opposed the reunion scheme. The local clergy clearly were both for joining together and lived in harmony until the opposition speakers, myself and the Voice of Methodism, did their best to destroy it and the meeting broke up in some disorder. Methodists generally saw their beloved chapels under threat because these would become redundant when the parish church became the centre of a united church – chapel buildings might become expendable but churches had to remain part of the Establishment.

So after a lengthy tour of the country it was clear to me that if the scheme was forced upon Christians at local levels, greater disunity would follow. Already a continuing Church of England was being planned and the same applied to dissident Methodists. Because Riley and Coleman supported the reunion scheme, Anglo-Catholics appeared uncertain and this gave rise to a new ultra-Catholic society, the League of Anglican Loyalists (LAL) supported by the head of the Society of the Holy Cross (SSC) Father Alfred Simmons and this was unfortunate because it divided Anglo-Catholics at a time when they needed to be united. A special Church Union general meeting was held in London to decide on future action. Father Coleman spoke in the morning about good points of the reunion scheme. At lunch I could see members were unhappy and in the afternoon I made a strong speech against the scheme and the meeting cheered and approved a statement for the Press expressing its opposition. Coleman was furious and said he could not possibly face reporters on the next day. I said I was happy to do so and as a result we made the headlines.

As the day for the final vote in the Church Assembly approached, it was impossible to forecast the result. Graham Leonard and I circulated a last-minute plea for the scheme's rejection. The scene in the Assembly was tense as we awaited the result. Methodists at their councils had approved the scheme by a small majority despite the fact that their members were against it and we wondered whether Anglicans would get the 75% required. They failed by a fair margin. Some unfeeling cad broke the stunned silence by clapping and was immediately silenced by a righteous 'shame'. When the new General Synod met a year or two later and voted again on the unaltered scheme it was defeated by an even greater number.

So ended a crisis which could have divided the Church of England and left it with an unholy mess. Despite the Church Union's final stand, it was weakened by early indecision and for the time being the LAL made the running. Bishops came badly out of the affair for most of them had voted for the reunion although some were doubtful. As one Catholic-minded bishop said to me, 'I voted for it because I knew it would not go through'; a foretaste of their later attitude in future debates, as we shall see.

While the Anglican/Methodist scheme was being debated in the Church Assembly, plans were being made to replace it with a General Synod. Dioceses were asked to discuss it and I set out once again to spell out the proposals to our members but they were too worn out by the heat engendered by the previous affair and I found it difficult to rouse any interest. I was alarmed by the details for new church government for they seemed to be heading for an ecclesiastical parliament where different parties of High, Low and Middle could be embattled. Matters of church faith, doctrine and practice could be decided and changed by members who could be governed more by emotion and churchmanship than by sound learning. It was true that the bench of bishops would have the final say in important changes but their behaviours in the Anglican/Methodist debate did not exactly give encouragement. A reluctance to overrule the lower houses of the Synod in the name of democracy could mean the surrender of episcopal authority to people power and this was contrary to the proud claim of the Church of England to be successors of the Apostles.

The misgivings which some of us felt when the proposals for a general synod were announced have been justified. At first the synod settled down to an orderly routine and everybody played the game but as the years have gone past precious articles of faith have been challenged or ignored. As we shall see later, the decline and fall of confidence in the Gospels under liberal scholarship has resulted in issues being decided in the light of appropriateness and expediency (words of J. L. Houlden) rather than by the authority of Christ.

Boat boy at St George's, Beckenham, 1923

With my parents at a cousin's wedding, 1937

Army chaplain, 1941–44

Naval chaplain, 1947–62

HMS *Mauritius* in Malta, 1949

With the Mountbattens on a visit to Tito, 1954

Master of St John's, Lichfield, 1982–92

After Confirmation by the Bishop of Lichfield

With Sisters of St Margaret, Colombo 1980

60th Anniversary of priesthood with my Bishop David Say at
St Barnabas, Beckenham

Bishop Martin Sigillito (left) with the Archbishop of Canterbury
and the Bishop of Quincy, USA

91 years old with friends

Chapter Ten

Putting the Laity in their Place

At the beginning of this book I said I had been lucky in my parents who were good churchgoing people. My father was more because he was both a leading layman and a good organiser. These he used for the benefit of our parish church in Beckenham, being a master of ceremonies and a group scout master. He was trusted by people inside and outside the church and was literally a friend of all. He was elected to the parish church council which was 'ruled' by an autocratic rector. This was the cause of endless frustration to him and he would return fuming after meeting because Father Francis Boyd had ridden roughshod over attempts by lay members to make their voice heard. In the end for peace of mind he retired from the council.

He did not know that he was in a long tradition of a two-tier membership of the Church, where the clergy ruled and lay people were seen but not heard. 'What are the laity for?' asked a Victorian dignitary, 'but to hunt, to shoot and to entertain. These matters they understand but to meddle in ecclesiastical matters they have no right at all.' Elsewhere a layman's duties were described as kneeling before the altar, sitting below the pulpit and putting his hand in his pocket!

It was not always so. In 1970 I wrote two booklets, *The Day Before Yesterday* and *Yesterday and Today* in which I showed the decline of the once proud status of Christian lay people to one of complete domination by the clergy. At one time in the Early Church they shared with priests in the mission and maintenance of the people of God. As an early Father of the Church taught there was a priesthood of the laity as priests, prophet and king (ruler) which stopped short of saying Mass and hearing confessions. As a result of this partnership the Church grew throughout the world to the extent that mission (except to the edges of the world) gave way to the organisation of the new members who were flooding into church buildings. It became a matter of providing Mass and the sacraments for large congregations and for this priests took pole position. Gradually lay people surrendered their rights as baptised Christians and were glad to let their priests do all the work. With the conversion of the Roman Emperor, Constantine in AD330 there came a parting of the ways for the Church. It could either continue along the path of the servant figure or could go the way of power and earthly distinction. The latter way was chosen and, in fact, it might have been difficult for the former way to be pursued without its becoming an insignificant sect. Some holy men read the sign of the times and departed for the deserts where they could continue in the poor tradition. For the rest the Church's choice showed itself in the magnificence of its buildings and extravagant ceremonial. The Bishop of Rome was promoted steadily in authority and rights and from him flowed the power of command through bishops, clergy and religious. These men decided all matters of faith and discipline. So the idea of the clergy and laity dressing alike and sharing alike in the running of Christ's family gave way to a situation where a few clergy made and enforced decisions and the majority had only to obey.

I have quoted considerably from my former essay, written when I was starting my campaign for the recovering of confidence for the lay ministry in a lay apostolate. It seemed our Church had to understand that we were now in the same position of early Christians when all hands were needed to bring converts into Catholic faith and practice. I even suggested that the prophetic ministry of teaching and preaching could be as important as that of celebrating the sacraments. This alarmed some of my fellow clergy and yet unless people are preached to and taught in church there would be no congregations for them to minster to. This surely was how the Early Church was formed and today we are in a similar mission situation; *Mission de Pays* was how France was described by one writer and England was in a similar position.

It was of course the lifestyle of the first Christians which caught the eye of others but this had to be followed up by a simple account of what Jesus said and did and this was recorded in the Gospels. I saw recently a question by a historian; how St Paul could afford to say so little about the life of Jesus in his letters and preaching unless there were written gospels available and this leads to the conclusion that they were available at an earlier rather than a later date. As I was promoting a lay apostolate in 1970 an Australian priest from Tasmania, Jim Cranswick, came into my office. He had been working on a theology of Christian formation which was found in St Paul's letters. When a person first believed, it was like a baby conceived in the womb and when it was born it needed gentle care and nourishment. So when a person was first accepted into the Church it was the job of the local community to surround him or her with loving care and attention as he or she was prepared for baptism, confirmation and first Communion. This was not just the work of a priest who was already overloaded with other chores. Trained lay people could provide hospitality, advice and even instruction if a teacher should be available. In many parishes there are often schoolteachers in the congregation whose expertise was being wasted.

Cranswick spoke to my growing apostolate at meetings and summer schools. I was invited with him to a conference in Madrid of priests who had left the official Roman Catholic Church in France, Belgium, Spain and other European countries and set up outposts for people in search of faith. Priests were there with lay apostolate teams and they welcomed an Anglican to their midst, helping me to come to terms with the difference of language. The atmosphere was full of happy enthusiasm as we discussed problems of interesting outsiders in France and Spain. There were many of these because of the split between Church and State going back to the French Revolution in the eighteenth century and to the Spanish Civil War in the twentieth. The break had never been healed with the result that many were born and brought up outside the Church. As I explained, the situation in Britain was different because Church and people co-existed happily, having drifted apart over the years but still maintaining a tenuous association in baptisms and church weddings.

Altogether it was an exciting week in this hostel run by Spanish nuns. I joined in the daily Mass and even celebrated with our new Series Two rite, at which all made their Communion, including a local bishop. We were able to see lay apostolate cells in action both in Madrid and Toledo and I noted that the Bible had a prominent place. I returned home very uplifted by what I had seen and heard but knowing that I had to adapt to our domestic situation. However, interest was being shown round the country and groups were registered at Church Union. It was clear that sound education was of prime importance and I set to work providing programmes for study. Knowledge of the Bible seemed a priority but here I ran into an Anglican difficulty. In the 1970s we were in the hands of radical New Testament critics who were phasing out the Gospel as guides to modern Christian living. It was unfortunate that two leading critics were Denis Nineham and Leslie Houlden for they were numbered among our Catholic scholars. The former was to become warden of Keble College, Oxford and the other principal of Cuddesdon Theological College, having been at one time principal of my old theological college, Chichester. At the first executive committee of the Church Union I attended in 1966 I had learned of the distance between pew and scholars but nobody seemed to identify this with New Testament waywardness. After all, as I said earlier the High Church movement had not been interested in the Bible, as being a Low Church preoccupation. In my year's theology at Cambridge before the war I had listened to the different theories about the formation of the Gospels but dismissed them as harmless playthings of scholars – after all they had to do something to earn their keep! Much later I discovered that these were not only the vagaries of the theological faculty but that they had taken hold of historians as well. In a very recent book on the history of Christ's College, Cambridge David Cannadine shows how the great modern historian, Jack Plumb, had accused historian academics of being more interested in ideas than adapting history to developing society, of being obsessed with scholarly technique. This was the problem with Anglican theologians.

It has been said that controversy is the breath of life to the German scholar and this certainly crossed the Channel to our academic circles. Theologians in Britain came to be described as 'first-class scholars doing third-class theology' and church life at local level suffered gradually by this isolation of theologian from the pew.

Fr Eric Mascall, a member of the Church Union Theological committee of which I was also a member, tried hard to stem the rush of religious lemmings over the cliff and his book *Theology and the Gospel of Christ* laid bare the depths into which theological thinking was sinking. In his autobiography, *Saraband*, published not long before his death he writes, 'for the Christian theologian is not merely someone who has been trained in a certain investigative method and then turned loose to practise it upon the documents and institutions of Christianity: he is – or should be – living and thinking and praying within a great tradition'. In a lecture in 1962 at King's College, London, he said, 'As I see it, the task of the Christian theologian is that of theologising – *theologizandum est in fide*; he may criticise contemporary expression of the tradition but like a good householder he will bring out of his treasure things new and old. But he will have no other gospel than that he has received.'

Mascall writes further: 'Throughout my active lifetime, however, the Church in all its branches has been subjected to a widespread and many-faced process of erosion of which the leaders have been largely unconscious and to which, even when they were conscious of it, they have often helplessly capitulated.'

I could not express better my experience in the early 1970s when I came to compose a year's course on the Bible for my increasing lay apostolate cells. I was dealing with lay people, most of whom had had a minimal instruction in the faith and who did not even understand the words which Christians use; in fact in the following year at a lay apostolate summer school on the south coast I was challenged to prepare a course on basic Christian belief. Meanwhile I composed a careful programme on the Bible, keeping clear of any ideas which might have caused alarm to tender minds. How right I was in the light of further developments, but more of that later!

Then for the fifth year, which proved to be my my last, I put together the required course on basic Christian words: Love, Salvation, Faith, Memorial and more which continues to be of interest after thirty years and which seems to show how much we have misjudged lay ignorance.

I had now done eight years at the Church Union and it was time to look for a final job. My championship of the laity had not been welcomed by some of the clergy, including members of the executive committee. I heard some priest saying, 'I am not going to let my congregation do my job', which indicated a complete misunderstanding of the lay apostolate strategy which was to take some of the load from the parish priest's workload. Lay people could reach areas of a parish which the vicar could not reach. Did not Vatican II say, 'Many people can only hear the gospel through the laity who live near them'? But the faithful churchgoer has to be trained before he is able to teach others and this was exactly the purpose for my lay apostolate strategy. It was in fact embedded in the ministry of the Early Christian Church and made possible a rapid extension into the heathen world. Unfortunately after I left it was allowed to lapse but the strategy has remained on the table for anyone who has my vision. It is all contained in a book I wrote some years ago, *A Church In Miniature* including material for basic teaching.

So regretfully I looked for another job. No Catholic parish was available – perhaps my ideas had been too dangerous! So I felt an urge or vocation to return to the teaching world. You may remember I had been a Classics teacher after the war and I knew Latin and Greek teachers were becoming difficult to find. I ended up first in a girls' Woodard school in the North but soon fell foul of the chapel mistress who invited me into her chapel to take such services she had arranged and approved of – something difficult to bear for one who had been in the forefront of liturgical change! I was unhappy in this women's world but was rescued by the headmaster of Roedean, the top girls' school.

I exchanged north for south and settled into a happy and interesting pre-retirement job in the twilight of my life, as I told my friends. Incidentally I was not the first older priest to take on such a job and I found it in some ways preferable than for a virile young man. I was head of religious studies as well as chaplain but found there was little evidence of definite Christian teaching. There were no Bibles to be found and no trace of a curriculum except for what I called a 'glossy' picture book which seemed to cover all religions generally. After a year finding my way I decided that a professional study of the Gospels was needed, tied to an exam if possible. So I launched into an O level course covering the first three Gospels, leading up to an exam for the Lower Vth. At first there were groans from the girls who had been using the Divinity periods for writing letters to their boyfriends or just taking time out and the headmaster was worried, too. However, I persevered and my classes began to accept the challenge if only because it gave them the experience of taking an O level a year before the rest. Soon I found even Hindus and Buddhists getting good passes. They used to crowd into my study before the exam and ask questions and I felt that even if it did not improve their spiritual life at least they had a basic foundation of gospel knowledge. I still have a letter from the headmaster, congratulating me!

This was praise indeed because at the end of my first year he had cast doubts on my teaching ability although he approved my efforts to improve chapel worship. But given a decent script I have always been able to put it over well. I had in fact only one period a week to prepare my classes for the O level exam over four terms and this needed planning. I prepared a series of notes on the gospel texts and had these printed off by a school secretary, Marion Banfield. So we followed each chapter using these notes which the girls could take away and study when doing their homework. After I retired I had them properly printed and turned into a small book which proved popular for teachers inside and outside school; I introduced the text by saying it was not meant to be a scholarly commentary but a work book.

I first noted the central theme of the Gospels which was the 'kingdom of God or heaven' which was a phrase well-known to Jews and for the most meant the spectacular and powerful invasion by God into a world where his chosen people, the Jews, had suffered considerably at the hands of the Gentiles. God would defeat these evil people and give a great celebration feast for his special people and then give them the kingdom for themselves. But Jesus taught another side to this kingdom of his Father. It would come only when everybody joined the fight against evil by showing love of God and neighbour – love was the key word instead of hate and confrontation. All could join this struggle, even sinners and Gentiles. This offended the religious authorities who believed only those who kept the Law would be rewarded. So they had no time for Jesus and finally killed him. I then continued with notes on what I considered difficult parts of the first three Gospels. Fortunately I had paid several visits to the Holy Land so I could give my classes a scenic background to enliven the lessons. So the scheme worked but unfortunately was dropped when I finally left. Only then could I approach the Gospels with greater confidence because challenges were being made to the radical critics by a new generation of New Testament scholars who were more conservative.

The other side to my work was the chapel worship. We had daily prayers in the huge chapel which seemed out of proportion to the rest of the buildings and could be fiendishly cold in the winter when the cold winds blew from the north. The Sung Eucharist was the main Sunday service and, with the help of a brilliant organist and music mistress, Janette Cooper, who was also a good churchwoman, could be very uplifting. Parents and friends were welcome so we could have over 400 in the congregation which posed a problem for giving Communion. It was possible with the help of local priests and in the end I evolved a plan by which girls helped themselves to the hosts from a ciborium and then received the chalice from me. I found myself ministering to a number of well-known parents, such as Lord Hailsham, Kenneth Baker, Freddie Laker, and others.

Generally Roedean was a worthwhile job although exhausting since there was also a constant stream of Confirmation candidates to prepare. Bishop Ambrose Reeves, who had been banished from his South African diocese for opposing apartheid, gave me help with their instruction. He had retired to Sussex and although he had had a stroke was still able to hold the girls' attention. He was, I suppose, seen as a martyr of a good cause and because we had a number of coloured girls he was held in great respect. When he died I took a party of girls to the memorial service in St Paul's Cathedral. I thought they might have been bored by the traditional ceremonial but instead they were overawed by the dignity of it all. This, and another episode, made me realise that we had been wrong in trying to bring down church worship to a popular level. It had been the school custom to have a house service on one Sunday of the month in place of the normal Sung Eucharist. Girls did their own thing with various performances, some clever, others scarcely religious at all. After some time I had a deputation from the girls to ask if we could return to the normal Eucharist. Yet I have seen the Church experimenting with all kinds of informal liturgies which fail to attract the young but upset the regulars. My long experience with young people has taught me that they expect to see dignity in worship. This should be a warning to some parish priests who no longer act with dignity at the altar and shamble into the sanctuary as if they are ashamed of their priestly vestments and liturgy. There is a time and place for informality but the parish Mass is not one of them. We come to pay our respectful duty to our Lord and Master and not to a social occasion and I believe most people expect it, especially in this chaotic world.

The time came for me to retire and I left the school with happy memories. Roedean girls are *sui generis* with glamour and comfort rationed in term-time and it produces strong characters – a gathering of old Roedeanians can be a fearsome sight! When I left I was made an Old Roedeanian, almost like a decoration for faithful service!

After I left the classroom I had time for reading and was able to catch up with what was happening in New Testament scholarship. If only I had known that the former radical and sceptical had become out of date I would have been a stronger and better teacher of religious studies!

In fact, I was not finished with education. I was invited to teach in a college of Further Education where I met mature students of all ages. By the time I finally retired I had taught pupils from eight to eighty, in both private and state education and so was able to form conclusions about its decline at classroom level. I believe teachers should come before their pupils having mastered the subjects they have to teach. The young soon know if a lesson has been badly prepared. Perhaps authority was weakened way back in the 1960s when a Labour government introduced pupil-centred education at the expense of the teacher who became little more than a manager or organiser.

PART THREE

Chapter Eleven

In Journeying Often

By courtesy of the Army and even more so of the Navy my experience of the wide world was considerably widened before tourism and industry swamped faraway places. As I have already described, Britain still governed countries in the east: Ceylon, Singapore, the Seychelles, and Mauritius, with India and Pakistan still in the Commonwealth. Oil had yet to transform sheikhdoms in the Persian Gulf into wealthy powers. When I was invalided from the Navy I thought I had said goodbye to travelling but when I had been in my Cornish parish for a year I saw an advertisement in the *Church Times* about a voyage of a lifetime organised by Inter-Church Travel. This had first been organised in the early 1960s by an Essex vicar, Arthur Payton who conceived the idea of taking church people of different denominations round the Mediterranean in a ship, spending a week in the Holy Land and visiting other exciting places. It was modestly priced at £100 for three weeks.

This seemed a good introduction to Israel which I had not visited before. So in the company of 400 pilgrims, bishops, priests and lay people, Catholic and Protestant, I took a train through France to Cannes where we boarded a Typaldos steamship and set sail for the Middle East. We were organised into small groups, each under an experienced leader. Our first stop was Beirut where we took taxis via Baalbek over the

desert to Damascus and then via Jordan to Jerusalem where
Palestinian guides took us round the Holy Places. This was in
1963 when the country was divided between Arab and Jew. So
we had to cross over into Israel through the Mandelbaum Gate
and so to Galilee where archaelogists were slowly uncovering
towns and villages of the first century AD. This was my first
sight of places I had read about in the Bible and it was very
exciting.

I enjoyed it so much that I went on two more voyages and
witnessed more excavations. I became a leader so had to pay
nothing. Altogether over the years I have led eight pilgrimages
and seen steady progress in digging up the past. In fact I have
learnt more about the land of our Lord than some New Testament scholars but more about that later. In the voyages we
included places like Ephesus, Istanbul, Mount Athos (men
only), Athens, even Rome where Pope Paul VI greeted us. I
took the author, Angela du Maurier, on one of the voyages
and she wrote a book, *Pilgrims by the Way*. Altogether it was
a great pioneering venture into the field of religious tourism
and should not be forgotten.

My travelling was by no means ended and I was given the
opportunity of returning to places I had know earlier. While I
was at Roedean I was asked by a conference of public school
chaplains to return to Sri Lanka to create a link with schools
there. I spent a month on the beautiful island and kept a diary
which shows how it had changed since 1950 when I lived
there.

Sri Lankan Diary July and August 1978

Tuesday 24 July
After a long flight we arrived in violent rain. We completed
landing formalities in a Turkish bath temperature. I was met
by Father Duleep de Chickera, a tall Sinhalese priest chaplain
of St Thomas's School, Mount Lavinia, with whom I had been
corresponding. As we drove twenty miles to Colombo I noted
little had changed or been repainted since 1951, our car
weaving through bullock carts, cows and pedestrians in

torrential rain. We drove first to meet the bishop, Swithun, in his new house beside his cathedral, a high and austere building next to the Palace of Unaligned Nations built by the Chinese for the strongly socialist prime minister Mrs Bandaranaike. Embarrassed by its proximity to the Christian cathedral a large modern Buddha was built opposite – overnight!

Then to Mount Lavinia on the coast and my lodging. I was lucky in my hosts, Alec Wigesinghe, a distinguished retired civil servant and former Sri Lankan cricket captain, and his wife Grace. Test matches were on at home and he and I listened to broadcasts on his ancient and unreliable radio.

The bad news is that I am to leave early tomorrow for five days in Jaffna, the northern tip of the island. Moreover there is a Tamil/Sinhala dispute over Tamil independence and I am warned about the TLF (Tamil Liberation Force) which was capable of IRA-type attacks.

Wednesday 25 July
Rose at 4 a.m., at Colombo Fort railway station by 5 a.m. in time to see a venerable set of coaches discharging loinclothed men of all ages clutching boxes, scales and sacks, off to collect fish for inland areas. My bearer, Kandy, was waiting and off we went.

The train journey was hard going. Lush vegetation gave way to scrub and flat sandy soil. An unending flow of men and boys sold almost everything. The train was behind time and I was hungry so I ate sandwiches left over from breakfast and gave the final remains to poor children beside the track. A generosity I was to regret.

The train then came to a sudden stop and after half an hour we learnt that the TLF had blown up the track, twenty-five miles short of Jaffna. Kandy carried my bags and we all deserted the train like rats and formed a long procession along the rails to the nearest station where we found confusion but no alternative transport. Kandy tried to phone the Archdeacon of Jaffna but Sri Lankan directories have their own peculiar system. We could not contact Archdeacon Hoskinson my host (in fact he was not on the phone) but at last spoke to St John's School in Jaffna and were promised someone would come. All this was done in a small post office where I made several friends chiefly by signs. Eventually an ancient taxi arrived driven by a cheerful young priest. The taxi was in some trouble with a steaming radiator and no handbrake. We made slow progress but finally arrived at 6.30 p.m. at the Archdeacon's house which was large and bare. The Archdeacon believed in holy poverty as an example to the world and I too was caught up in it. However he and I drove almost immediately to dinner with a Jaffna University professor and another from Hawaii – very pious! Then to bed in a sort of outhouse exposed on all sides. All kinds of animal noises but I was too tired to mind.

Tuesday 26 July
Not a bad night but warm. A dawn chorus of birds awakened me and after a simple breakfast I was off to St John's School for daily service in chapel. I gave of my best to 200–300 children for thirty minutes and then found only half could understand English!

Next to Nuffield (in name only) Deaf and Dumb School where Javasingh David, an amazing man in his forties, was the headmaster. He gave up a good job at St Thomas's School, Mount Lavinia, went to England and America and leant techniques for training deaf and dumb children, then returned to Jaffna and by training his own staff built up an efficient unit in very restricted buildings. Teachers also acted as matrons for boarders. He gave us a very Indian meal and indeed I was to live on native food for much of my tour. I left with the feeling that here was saintly man.

Then to Jaffna College, a Church of South India school, of 1000 pupils (260 Christians). I spoke in an excellent hall to senior pupils and staff and apparently struck the right note; the importance of religious studies. This subject is now re-emerging after a difficult time under a former Communist regime. Here a very minority Christian population has had great influence through the education programme of the last century.

The Archdeacon told me that in 1826 a Rev Joseph Knight came to Jaffna. He learnt Tamil from a Brahmin priest who after each lesson had to go home and bath to wash off the defilement of mixing with a foreigner. Knight started a school and the work continues.

In a short time I began to feel materialism was catching up with this island and warned that with the coming of television they were becoming part of a global village. Many belong to the Christian Church to show they are neither Buddhist or Hindu. To be without a religion would isolate – it was a question of identity.

I found myself at tea after my talk with a kindly and elderly bearded Hindu teacher who wondered at the wisdom of teaching the Synoptic Gospels – three versions. He had little to say about his faith except that he followed the faith of his family and believed in an ultimate god or gods. This vagueness belonged to the Buddhists, so the Archdeacon told me. They are far from hidebound. While things are going well – the wheel of cause and effect smoothly turning – they are good Buddhists, but in a crisis they turn to some power above, a Hindu god, a Christian god or even one of the saints like St Anthony. When things return to normal they are Buddhist again. The difference between Hindu and Buddhist apparently is that a Hindu believes in reincarnation of self in another form, a Buddhist only in reincarnation – not the same self reborn. These philosophies are based on an idea of a world which is ugly and unpleasant. I wondered how this conception would change if the welfare state transformed society.

After all this talk I was worn out – after all I had only been in this country for two days but my man Kandy looked after me very well. Back to a native meal; curry.

Friday 27 July
An excellent night's sleep for the first time. Then we made our precarious way to the Roman Catholic church, St Anthony's, where I was to address all the local clergy on 'The Priesthood Today'. I should say that all rides in the Archdeacon's ancient Fiat 500 were fraught with danger for he drove

on any empty patch on the road and also because he had no handbrake, as he said 'handbrakes are unnecessary on flat Jaffna roads'! After a year he had also failed to get his bearings so he would constantly lose his way home. All the time he nattered away in a fast Indian-flavoured English.

The Roman Catholics did us well. Among the Christians they predominate because for many years the island was colonised by the Portuguese. I spoke to a varied set of clergy: Roman Catholics, Anglicans, Church of South India, Methodists chiefly on the themes of my essays, *The Day Before Yesterday* and *Yesterday And Today*. This provoked a great discussion about leadership and joy etc., not least about the problem of English. The Archdeacon described the situation: 'The English missionaries came, built a church and school, surrounded them with a wall then invited natives to leave their past life and join the English.' This often meant promotion under the British Raj. The Roman Catholic charismatic priest mentioned the higher standard of the clergy and the unfair advantage it gave them over their flock. He thought evangelism was slack because efforts were being directed from the centre to making people better Buddhists and Hindus. He suggested they should follow the Eastern teaching of immanence. Later he took me into his church and showed me how to reverence the altar in the Eastern way.

The Roman Catholic clergy had put on a good native lunch of which I enjoyed small curried crabs the most. It was odd to see the clergy and even higher layers of society eating with their fingers, mixing delicately and blending different spiced dishes. Incidentally the Roman Catholic priest told me that less and less confessed their sins privately but preferred group confession.

In the evening I gave a public lecture on evangelism in a dimly lit hall to an audience of about fifty people. I spoke about lay responsibility, a message much needed, I gathered.

Jaffna was almost all Tamil and therefore Hindu. There was a magnificent temple which was being prepared for a local occasion. Hinduism flourishes on festivals of local gods who are carried in procession. The Archdeacon remarked 'religion easily becomes the marrying of gods to man's convenience'.

We agreed that the acquiring of merit haunts most religion. Christians have done it but Hindus and Buddhists carry out ceremonies to give them advantage in any reincarnation. I should note here that the Roman Catholic church we visited this morning cashed in on loudspeaker canned music and blasted forth religious pop music from its tower. It was strange to hear Marian hymns competing with profane jazz.

Saturday 28 July
Another good night despite the sound of strange animals running along the rafters. I was not reassured by the mention of scorpions and snakes at the breakfast table. On the way to my morning session we passed preparations for a Hindu festival. I noticed a number of men carrying coconuts in their hands, some obviously on fire. I was told that it was a custom to throw these before one of the many images of gods on the outside of temples. It was a symbolism, the white flesh of a coconut indicated a pure heart, broken pieces a surrender of self and a burning coconut a heart aflame with love. A sort of sacramental, I suppose, but inconvenient to be practised in a Christian church – too messy by far!

I spoke to an audience chiefly of teachers on the lay apostolate and this made an impact. There was an unfortunate attempt to intrude Bible fundamentalism. In the afternoon I met young people who asked about youth in England, witchcraft and black magic (topical because an Anglican priest, Father Peiris awaits trial on a charge of murder connected with the occult). Since he was a Sinhalese I suppose the Tamils enjoyed the discomfiture! The young people sang beautifully to a guitar which indicated a touch of the charismatic.

The Archdeacon and his family have been housing me and since they believe that the clergy should as far as possible share the native lifestyle our food was chiefly simple, rice served with a few spiced dishes.

Sunday 29 July
As a climax to my stay in Jaffna I preached at the 7 a.m. parish Eucharist at St John's. The vicar is Father Joseph

Sarvananthan, a Catholic with Reservation. The Eucharist however was simple: surplice and stole. The first part was in Tamil (except the sermon when I preached on the words memorial and liturgy). I then took over the prayer of thanksgiving to the end. The church was crowded and many made their Communion. Some saluted the host in Eastern fashion before receiving, a growing practice on the island and a good one. Afterwards I was given a good English breakfast and then Kandy and I caught the noon train to Colombo. The journey back was long, uncomfortable and crowded but not eventful. I had time to reflect on the first part of my tour.

I found little feeling about independence among the Tamils I met and no violence. They differ from the Sinhalese further south. The latter call them mean but I would say they watch their money carefully. There is something of the Scot in them. The flat dry dusty land seems to have produced a hard-working austere people in contrast to the more volatile Sinhalese who live more among lush vegetation. I was puzzled by the CSI (Church of South India). We are in communion with them and yet there seemed few signs of a growing together of CSI and Anglicans. There was a CSI bishop and a cathedral in Jaffna despite the fact that the Anglican Bishop of Colombo has jurisdiction over that area. In fact they appear to be expanding their Church into Colombo itself. In other words we have created another church, some of whose members, Methodists and Baptists, do not seem eager for closer ties. CSI has strong backing of American money and some hard-liner southern Baptists had recently moved into the area. I found an interesting lesson here for union schemes at home.

I was met at the Fort station by Duleep. Colombo as usual was a seething mass of humanity. I had a few hours' sleep at my guest house at Mount Lavinia.

Monday 30 July
On the morning train for Gurutalawa in the hills in the company of a young Sinhala David Amarasake, an Old Thomian. The train began a slow ascent to the hills, a journey I would have enjoyed had I not done twenty hours of train

journey in the days before. It was good to see the tea plantations again. The prospect of cooler weather was a relief
although it turned out warm and rainy. We arrived at Haputale
and I was able to see the age of the carriages which brought
back memories of the former British Raj but alas there were
no amenities such as dining cars which I remembered served
an excellent evening meal in the 1950s. Transport was waiting
and we were soon at St Thomas's, a smaller version of the
school at Mount Lavinia. The headmaster was Sinhala and
looked formidable at first but proved to be an excellent
companion. He had taught in Kent at home. He kept me
talking about Bible criticism at supper with others joining in
well beyond the meal. There is a language problem for the
boys here because the younger ones were trying to catch up on
their English and so only the older ones could understand my
talks. The socialists government had stopped the teaching of
English for a generation and then had to restart it because it
caused problem with a growing tourist trade.

A good night's sleep under sheets and blankets.

Tuesday 31 July
John Marasinghe, a good Christian and wildlife expert took
me to the beautiful Horton Plains. We were unlucky with the
weather and rain sent us home, but only after we had seen
monkeys and jungle birds. In the evening I spoke to some
boys and staff in the beautifully equipped chapel.

Wednesday 1 August
A lovely warm morning. The birds are a delight; 120 vari-
eties. A green woodpecker eats figs outside my window. I was
given a tour of the school by a member of the staff. The boys
run their own savings bank and farm. The local state school is
very bad – the headmaster comes in only twice a week. So
there is an incentive to try to send children to independent
schools. The country is in fact trying to raise the standard of
education and even in socialist days of the Bandaranaike
regime every effort was made to keep private schools. Most of
the ministers come from them. I found the young very cynical

about their politicians. Whoever offers the most to the poverty-stricken will have power.

At 6.30 in the evening Christian staff came to the head-master's house and kept me busy answering questions about youth in England. I spoke from a general experience and said frustration and apathy were the chief enemies, leading to vandalism and stealing. Nearly two hours!

Wednesday 2 August
Another beautiful morning but the vagaries of the weather in this area were shown when we went to Nuware Eliya, twenty miles as the crow flies only to find a drenching, continual downpour. We visited the Paynter Home, started many years ago for the children of English planters and their native women folk. This need has now faded but other unwanted children are now cared for. The house was decrepit, unmaintained, cold and damp and one wondered about the fortitude both of the children and their guardians. The chief organiser and his assistant had both left that morning for a holiday in England and the local staff were obviously overwhelmed by our invasion although they had been warned. I gave a short talk and then we left and found the sun shining back in Gurutalawa. But my heart grieved at the young derelicts in that home.

Friday 3 August
Up at 5.30 a.m. and caught the 8 a.m. train from Haputale with David and Prian. Very slow progress and overcast most of the way until we ran into the humid heat of Colombo. Back to the Wijesinghes for few days. I did some jewel buying in the evening with Mrs W's help.

Saturday 4 August
At last a free day at Mount Lavinia. I had a gorgeous swim in the surf although the undercurrent was strong. Too many beggers. It was interesting to watch trains passing at the back of the beach with people packed inside and others hanging on the outside. It was the same with buses. Our transport prob-

lems at home would be quickly solved if we allowed such overcrowding! Fares are cheap: 7p for a seven-mile trip, 50p for a seven-hour journey to the hill country.

At last I was able to take stock of the Sri Lanka situation. True, I had only been to unusual places like Jaffna in the north and the hills but Alec W. was well able to discuss the general situation over a glass of whisky or gin. With the withdrawal of the British in 1958 the country had tried to go it alone, finally falling into the hands of extreme socialists, even Communists. The economy quickly worsened, not helped by a mini civil war in the 1960s and three droughts in succession. The British tea planter with his 'Creepers' and large plantation was replaced by a system of cooperatives which ran it less economically. Nobody was allowed to own more than 50 acres. No new cars were allowed to be imported and this explains the ancient but well-polished minis and Austins which fill the roads. One can only wonder at the endurance of the old Morris 1000! Communist regimes have tried to cash in on the island's problems but I guess have retired, defeated by Sinhalese easy-going philosophy. I would think that the island has suffered by not having a supporting power. After all, for the last three hundred years it has had the Portuguese, the Dutch and the British to organise it. The last clearly did the best job and discerning Sinhalese know it. The trouble is that there are too few leaders and everything has slumped and stagnated. I suspect Alec has only a small pension despite his distinguished service. They subsidise this by running a pleasant guest house near Mount Lavinia. His car is an Austin Cambridge of the mid 1950s. Only recently has it been possible to import new cars.

The stagnant economy has made any promising young scholar or citizen seek for better things abroad. The result is that graduates of Sinhalese or Indian universities migrate to gain higher qualifications abroad and competent artisans are recruited by oil sheikhs in the Gulf. They earn vast sums and return comparatively wealthy men. This is not the recipe for a successful developing nation.

Generally one misses the Eastern music which once wailed

over populated areas. Today it is universal pop. The Roman
Catholic church I visited in Jaffna attempted to counter this
secular sound. St Anthony's blasted out religious music
including hymns to our Lady from its church tower and
nobody else was able to drown it.

Sunday 5 August
Started with a power blackout and pouring rain. This did not
discourage a large congregation at St Francis's, Mount Lavinia.
I preached by candlelight at 7 a.m. The vicar gave me breakfast
in his vicarage but I do dislike 'hoppers'; fried eggs in the
middle of a pancake. I then went to St Thomas's school chapel
to conduct a short retreat for Confirmation candidates – fifteen
boys and one girl. In the evening in the superb school chapel we
had a lovely evensong for the patronal festival of the Transfigu-
ration. The music was excellent but more memorable was the
sermon in the form of a dialogue in which two boys and two girls
took part. A son had graduated at the local university and
mother and father wondered how he would use his success.
Would he help with the education of his younger brothers and
sisters? But he is set on bettering himself abroad. It is left to his
girlfriend to persuade him that his talents as a teacher were
needed in his own country. It became a debate in which the use
of ability was set against vocation within the Church. It was well
worked out and mirrored Sri Lanka's need for responsible citizens.

Monday 6 August
Concelebrated with Bishop Swithun at the 7 a.m. Mass and
Confirmation. It was beautifully carried out and typical of the
island's sense of worship. There was a large breakfast afterwards which included sandwiches and cakes. The rest of the
day was a holiday and I was able to bathe in the evening when
the rain had stopped.

Mrs W. has Anglicised her meals very well despite the standard diet of rice with curries, made chiefly from fish with
occasional meat stews flavoured with chillies and spices. Fruit
of course is plentiful and delicious. I suppose expensive hotels

provide a wider diet but they cost £30 for a bed alone per night. Government guest houses are better value. I still found it difficult to accept the habit of eating with one's fingers even in the higher levels of society but I was assured that was a vital element in blending different spices of the local food.

I could not help feeling that the island could be ripe for a savaging by the secular west. At present television exists but only for three hours a day and I could not believe that this ration could exist for long; soon the full weight of western life would be thrown against what was still mostly a simple way of life. I did my best to warn audiences to be alive to this danger.

Tuesday 7 August
Today was *Poya* or full moon day and therefore a Buddhist general public holiday. This was supposed to celebrate Buddha's birth, enlightenment and death. Quiet music was played all day. Everything was closed except the zoo. The manager of this was Charles de Alwis, a member of Christ's College Cambridge, my old college, and I was given a conducted tour. It was a lovely setting and very clean. I watched a dance of the elephants and then was given tea in the VIP lounge.

Wednesday 8 August
Tour of St Thomas's School which has 2000 boys of which over half are Christian. For a century this school has been a great influence in the island. The chaplain, Duleep de Chickera, is a man of great ability and social concern. He has organised clinics in local slum areas. He worked on a budget of a thousand rupees a month (£35) which is raised by staff and boys. Drugs were bought, doctors give their services and boys assist. Local ladies have sewing classes and make clothes for poor children.

After this I took a bus to the Fort. What a shock! Traffic, vendors and crowds made progress difficult. Shops had fallen on evil days – no longer the elegant and fashionable stores where naval wives used to buy beautiful silks to be turned into dresses cheaply by local tailors. Then back in the overflowing bus.

Thursday 9 August
Wakened with tummy pains which persisted all day – must have been something I ate! However managed to tape the school choir and had dinner with the warden.

Friday 10 August
At 7.40 a.m. I preached at the end of term service at St Thomas's, then lectured for one and half hours at the Methodist Ladies College in Colombo, staff and girls, some Anglicans and found it tough going. Only real questions came from the staff, asking me to explain the Trinity! Pupils in senior classes seemed to understand English but found it difficult to articulate questions.

Visited St Margaret's Convent where I am to conduct a retreat a few days later. This convent's mother house is in East Grinstead where my daughter had been at school. Spoke to the chaplain, Fr Amarasake, who is a keen ecumenist but Christian unity is not an easy or safe matter.

In the afternoon there was a meeting of school chaplains at Christ Church Galle Face and the idea of an organised body joined with public schools in Britain was approved. Question arose about many lay people who do most of the Christian teaching in school.

Saturday 11 August
Further ordeal by train. Rose at 4.15 a.m. and was taken to the Fort to join Colombo contingent of youth for a conference at Gurutalawa in the hills. So-called special carriages on the train had obviously been brought out of long retirement. Seats were wooden, broken and contained bugs. I was still off-colour and would gladly have opted out of this excursion. It was a slow journey to the hills but the young were undaunted and endlessly sang good old English favourites. I was joined by a young priest, Russell Rebart, whom I had met the day before. I had put him down as an Evangelical but he was far from that. Realising my past connection with the Church Union he poured out the troubles of Catholics. Churchmanship had been watered down and a Methodist reunion scheme

hovered over them. He said there were other like-minded priests going to the conference so I arranged to meet them.

We limped our way via Kandy to Nanoya where we waited for one and a half hours for a connecting train to Haputale. I was fascinated to watch a family eat their packed meal in Nanoya waiting room. A curry meal had been packed in a dried plantain leaf then wrapped in newspaper. The leaf was unfolded and the meal eaten with fingers. Apparently this system keeps the food warm. In some parts of the island plantain leaves are used instead of plates and then thrown away to prevent other castes from using the same plate.

We finally reached Haputale and then had to wait for buses to take us the rest of the way. Two-hour wait. I was now desperate with tiredness. It was over twelve hours since we started our journey. Finally buses arrived and hurtled us round hairpin bends so violently that our radiator gave out but fortunately in sight if St Thomas's Gurutalawa. I made for the headmaster's house to find a drinks party in full swing. It had been prizegiving and some governors and old boys had stayed behind. I had a hot bath, the only place during my travels I had such a luxury – bathrooms generally are much neglected and squalid places. I then joined the party where I was cross-questioned about education and other matters. A voluble Muslim – most were Christian – showed some ignorance of the Christian faith and thought Jesus belonged to the Old Testament. He thought Buddhism was the only religion which showed compassion. He was soon corrected by other members of the party. So to bed at 11.30 p.m. after a long day.

Sunday 12 August
Recovered enough to go to the 7 a.m. Mass concelebrated by mostly Catholic priests – first part in Sinhala and Tamil, second in English. Impressive singing and devotion by the young congregation. Then a quiet day.

Monday 13 August
Youth conference continued and I took park in English group discussions. Young men discussed the ideal wife separately

and the girls the ideal husband . . . then they joined together. One young man said he wanted a wicked wife but we felt he meant colourful. Most wanted a Christian partner. I was asked to sum up.

In the afternoon eight Catholic priests came to discuss the way forward. I suggested a renewal campaign and this was accepted. I felt a new beginning had been made.

The Bishop of Colombo, Swithun, arrived in the evening.

Tuesday 14 August
The excellent conference continued, led by a forceful Roman Catholic nun. It was a morning of self-examination! How do others see me? Who am I? The sister summed up well. We project ourselves in the best possible way so that we may be accepted. I was a group leader in a discussion on maturity.

A lunch party was given by the headmaster for the bishop and clergy. Once again it was strange to see almost all the party eating with their right hands – the left was used for less worthy functions. Here I should say it is difficult to get toilet paper; small bowls and water are provided but I did get some Kleenex tissues. After tea the sister gave an expert talk on the mechanics of sex to the English group with broad-minded advice on contraception.

Then at 6.45 p.m. an almost unbelievable climax to the conference – a pontifical High Mass (I was deacon and MC) with all the trimmings. The bishop preached in three languages and this took time. After Mass there was procession of the Blessed Sacrament through the grounds, girls danced exquisitely in front scattering petals as they went and Fr Cobban-Lea censed almost everything and everybody! Hundreds followed with lighted candles attracting tropical insects in the night air. Benediction was given and all went away in high spirits although some more sober-minded Tamils were overwhelmed, I heard.

Wednesday 15 August
By first-class observation car back to Colombo – the best train journey yet. Then to the convent and Mass of the Assumption.

Thursday 16–Monday 20 August
Conducted a retreat for the community of St Margaret. Two addresses each with Mass in the morning and Benediction at night. After a day I developed a rash on my backside after sitting on a convent cane chair. One of the sisters took me to the local surgery where a jovial large doctor said, 'You have the bugs, Father,' and gave me some ointment. The offending chair was quickly removed.

Preached at St Michael's Colombo. How standards have dropped since I conducted the marriage of a fellow naval officer there. The retreat ended after Terce and the sisters gathered to give their thanks. One of the sisters showed me something of the vocational work done for young men in book-binding and catering. The community also has rooms for women teachers, something much needed in this poor district of Polwatte.

Tuesday 21 August
My last day. A lovely walk in the sun from the Fort to Galle Face. Then by bus back to Mount Lavinia for a bathe and lunch with the de Chickeras. They are a youngish couple with small children. Duleep who organised my tour efficiently is obviously a priest with a future and I promised to try to try to get him a place for a course at Oxbridge – which in fact took place.

After farewells, to the airport and a night flight home via Zurich.

I left behind a month's hard work mostly creating a link between British and Sri Lankan Christians. This was very necessary because so little is known about them. I wondered about the future of the island. They really need in-depth leaders in all fields of national life. For this they need money for training abroad and this is not available. Extreme socialism is not keen on competition.

One left with a picture of several Ceylons. On the surface life continued at a leisurely pace. People of any social status at all still had their servants; unemployment would rise rapidly if they did not. There were the very poor, many of them beggars. There were labourers in the paddy fields and plantations. Tamil and Sinhala was spoken and a certain amount of English but the teaching of this had been somewhat neglected. In the tropical lowlands malaria could still be caught but in the highlands the climate was almost English. Unfortunately there were few in control of these elements. I felt they were at the mercy of any invading power but who would want this island in today's global strategy? I was left with the sight and sounds of many beautiful birds which were an unfailing source of delight: orioles, woodpeckers, minah birds and parrots, not forgetting the continued croaking of the crows.

Fifteen years later I returned to start a branch of the Cambridge Society. I was met by doctor, Joe Paul, who had been at Trinity with Prince Charles and was the leading heart specialist in the island. This time it was a non-religious occasion and I stayed in a luxurious hotel near Galle Face. Life generally seemed to have changed little except the traffic which had grown enormously, filling the main roads with cars ancient and modern and *bajajes*, three-wheeled taxis which clogged the streets but were cheaper. With the help of a friendly Chinese restaurant owner Joe and I arranged a thoroughly English tea party with cucumber sandwiches in the British Council centre. Joe warned me that some graduates might be too scared to come because Oxbridge men and women were not popular with the very socialist government. So on a very warm Saturday afternoon in Colombo we waited anxiously. By 3 p.m. only one, a Roman Catholic priest, had appeared but one by one others began to arrive, greeting me by their name and college and soon the hall was filled with Cambridge men and women. I explained what the society could offer them and what they could do for their old university, even helping young Sri Lankans to get there. Afterwards we had a jolly tea party and young and old shared experiences. A new branch of the society was formed so I felt my mission was accomplished. Despite some difficulties it has continued to flourish. I had some contact with the local government and was taken over by a Hindu lady official who at first showed an aggressive authority often typical of women in power, but later mellowed and even invited me to supper in her home.

She apparently was under the influence of her priestly guru who told her how to conduct her life. He told her to wear red and even get rid of her car. I wondered how much such superstition controlled other officials and even the very socialist government itself. It seemed a long way from the old days of the British Raj!

During my time at Roedean the Bishop in Europe asked if I could fly out to Prague to take Christmas services for the British community. It was 1979 and Communists were still ruling the country so it would not be entirely a holiday. I packed my bags and flew with my wife into Prague airport which was ringed by tanks and military. An official car was waiting for us and without any trouble drove us to the British Embassy where we were to stay with the ambassador and his wife, John and Rosemary Rich, who were both good church people. The Embassy itself was the former Thun Holenstein Palace, a beautiful and historic building. The lounge where Mozart had once composed part of his opera *Don Giovanni* was especially elegant. A formidable old wall protected the whole complex. There was no Anglican church so we had to set up the cinema for Christmas services. It was a day or so before the festival and we were able to have a conducted tour of the city which was full of history. It was a thrill to be walking in the same street and the beautiful square where great composers like Brahms, Smetana and Dvořák had once lived but the atmosphere generally was grim and gloomy. Many years of Communism had reduced citizens to a silent servility and both housing and food were in short supply. However they had been allowed to have their traditional Christmas Eve dish of carp and the fish were for sale, still swimming in baths in the market. Nobody spoke to us. Grey-faced they pushed their way past us but the beautiful buildings more than compensated for this behaviour. My mind went back several years when my naval ship was the first to go behind the Iron Curtain in Poland where even harsher conditions subdued the people.

On Christmas Eve I visited a grey apartment block where embassy personnel were housed and I managed to conduct a carol service. Later we had Midnight Mass in the cinema and many people came, including some Christians from other embassies. Vestments and altar vessels were brought from a store and we were able to have a dignified Mass with multiracial communicants. Later a small party sat down to Christmas dinner in the elegant dining-room which over the centuries had seen many celebrations. Food had been supplied from the embassy in Vienna and I must say it was one of the most sumptuous meals I have ever enjoyed. Conversation flowed freely until we were warned by signs that everything was probably heard by sophisticated hearing devices outside which could penetrate even strong walls. On Boxing Day, the feast of Stephen, we took a walk in the snow past St Agnes's Fountain which reminded us of a certain good King Wenceslaus who had walked this way. We spent a few days in the house of the Air attaché who lived on the edge of the city. Here security was even stricter because the boilerman who lived in the basement was known to be a communist mole. Some years later after the liberation I returned in a Cambridge tour party and found people beginning to enjoy their freedom. The police particularly had to do a volte-face and instead of being a much feared repressive force had now to become everybody's friend. It was the same in a new East Germany where fear was lifted but the people still had to overcome many years of occupation and to begin to think and speak for themselves.

Earlier, I described my first three visits to the Holy Land; since then I have led five more pilgrimages taken by plane. For most it was an impressive, even emotional experience, especially when we followed our Lord's last days in Jerusalem. Bethleham, too, they found moving especially when we knelt in a cave under the very old church and sang, 'O come all ye faithful', before the place of Jesus's birth. But this town became dangerous as fighting between Jews and Arabs intensified.

The Holy Places in the south of Israel have always drawn a constant stream of pilgrims and much work has been done to restore them. I became increasingly interested in the excavations going on in the north, in Galilee, which certainly from Victorian times has been depicted as a quiet countryside where shepherds and farmers worked undisturbed. Archaeologists are today revealing a different scene of a busy cosmopolitan life where considerable building accommodated foreigners who wanted to settle there. A great city, Sepphoris, had been rebuilt only a short distance from Nazareth where Jesus was growing up and possibly supplied work for him and Joseph. Every time I visited all this excavating activity I found more material for re-thinking about the writing of the Gospels until with the help of writers like Robinson, Mascall and Moule I was in a position to challenge the radical New Testament scholarship of men like Nineham and Houlden who had an unfortunate influence within our modern-day Church. This has provided me with employment for my retirement and I was lucky enough to be offered a job and accommodation where I could continue my studies.

Chapter Twelve

In Search of a Perfect Solution

The Church is like a flourishing country, which needs to have a good supply of water running through it from a spring in the hills, and allowed to flow freely until it becomes a large river. Stop that flow and the river turns first to a marsh and finally disappears. So the Church has functioned in a similar way when it has allowed the spring of revelation brought by Jesus to flow uninterrupted through the world, giving spiritual life to many. When this flow has been blocked or neglected the Church has dried up and become ineffectual. Many would see that this has happened in our day. Well did Jeremiah in the Old Testament complain, 'My people, says the Lord, have committed two evils for they have forsaken me, the fountain of living water and dug out cisterns for themselves, cracked cisterns which can hold no water.' Their God had been neglected for other gods leading to disaster and exile. So, in our country the revelation of God brought by Jesus has been rejected and other gods of money, pleasure and sex have taken over . . .

As I have said, I had been brought up in better days when sound teaching could still be found. Anglo-Catholics have been accused of neglecting the Scriptures between the wars but this was not true of my church. Great care was taken to teach children about the greatness of God, the helplessness of man and the saving revelation brought by Jesus and recorded faithfully in the Gospels. Simple stories supported by a system of stamps left us with a good knowledge of the ministry of Jesus. This was balanced by a dignified and magnificent worship at Mass where only the best was good enough for God.

All this excited me from my earliest days and by the time I reached my teenage years I was able to take my share of teaching in the Sunday school. As I have said a basic faith has remained with me throughout my many adventures. This faith has been kept alive by sound books and teachers. Only recently I read a book by a Greek monk who explained the gap between correct Christian belief and uninformed non-belief. The relationship between God and man had been misunderstood. God had been seen as an immovable object and man as the seeker. In fact it is man who by his limited nature is stationary and God is the one who moves out toward man seeking his love. I suppose this sums up my early conclusions and it has helped when considering modern scholarship and has kept me on the side of orthodoxy.

This has been essential for the other side of my life – education. Wherever I have settled I have found people who have needed to be taught simply. Although I have never had that training which is required of teachers today, I have been accepted in the teaching profession and even been thrown into the deep end. For example, at the end of the war after my invaliding from the Army, instead of returning to parish life, I was offered the job of senior Classics master in a public school. Because I had a Cambridge degree in the subject, I was taken on trust and had to get a number of boys through their O levels. Latin was still a required subject for the main universities. In addition I taught English so there was little time for religious studies which the headmaster, Tom Nevill, taught. However this first professional teaching post gave me confidence for future teaching because I had some success in getting pupils through their exams and I found I had an ability for communication. This included the gift of empathy by which I could feel what was in my pupils' minds; an essential quality for a teacher. Even in the Navy I found plenty of scope for teaching for it is keen on its religion and insists that its recruits should should be given regular instruction by chaplains. As I wrote earlier HMS *Ganges* gave plenty of opportunity for teaching the faith but it had to be done very simply. The chief need was introducing the boys to the Bible and there was certainly no place for theological speculation. In fact in all my parish instruction I have found that ignorance of the Christian faith is abysmal.

It was a different matter when I became a secretary in the Church Union which has always had a reputation for good scholarship and I felt everything I wrote and said would be carefully scrutinised. It was when I was composing a programme of learning for my lay apostolate that I sensed I had to be especially careful when I came to the study of the Bible, in the light of negative scholarship. This also applied to my teaching at Roedean and in a simple commentary I prepared for O level gospel study. I had to pull my punches, as it were, and this left me with a dissatisfaction with my performance.

As I look back I realise I should have had the courage of my convictions but my year reading theology at Cambridge had made me in awe of top scholars. These were a class on their own who lived in ivory towers which they left to give the benefit of their wisdom to lesser beings like myself. To challenge this could bring a pitying remark such as, 'it wasn't as simple as that' but my belief in the Gospels was uncomplicated for it seemed to me that if they were untrustworthy we had no Christian faith at all. The Christ of history disappeared and we were left only with the Christ of faith and this excluded a bulk of unlearned believers. I could understand there might be differences in ideas about the 'how' the Gospels were written but the 'what' of the Gospels had to remain inviolate. I did not realise that while I was teaching in the classroom scholars were steadily undermining the facts of our Lord's life and teaching. Only when I had left the classroom and was in retirement did I read Adrian Hastings' summing up of the 1960s and 70s in his masterful book, *English Christianity from 1920–90.*

Of the 1960s he wrote

A good deal of the more publicized theological writings in the sixties gives the impression of a surge of feeling that in the modern world, God, religion, the transcendent, any reliability in the gospels, anything which formed part of the old 'supernaturalist' system had suddenly become absurd ... At times it looked as if the authority of the Bible, the Church, scholastic theology and Christian spiritual experience were being rejected as 'irrelevant' and outdated to leave as the new sources of enlightenment little more that sociology, linguistic analysis, modern Marxism or the study of other religions.

When he came to write about the 1970s the situation had worsened:

This was in part because of the ever-increasing scepticism which the leading theologians of the English academic school – Dennis Nineham, Maurice Wiles, John Hick and others – were evincing in regard to all the central dogmas most characteristic of Christianity, the incarnation, the Trinity, even for some the very existence of God. It was most in evidence in relation to Christ. 'Is it any longer worthwhile,' asked Nineham, the urban doyen of the school, 'to attempt to trace the Christian's ever changing understanding of his relationship with God directly back to some identifiable element in the life, character and activity of Jesus of Nazareth?

In other words, it is no longer helpful to try to model your religious experience on the life of Jesus in the Gospel.

Hastings continues by saying that although the writings of this school provoked much excitement and discussion at the time they were not major works. An over-confident 'debunking' of the Incarnation in a book, *The Myth of God Incarnate*, was 'unpleasing' but it hastened the end of historic Christianity. A 'white flag was hoisted above the long-beleagured citadel of Christian belief causing a stunned excitement of the rank and file of weary defenders on learning that their staff officers had so light-heartedly ratted on them', (Hastings). A coup de grâce was given when some of these critics stated that it was impossible for modern man of the twentieth century to understand the culture of the first century AD anyway; a conclusion which I as a classical scholar could not accept.

The unhappy result of all this was that the figure of a divine Jesus began to fade out of the teaching world inside and outside church. The gospel accounts of our Lord's ministry were reduced to a minimum in schools, even in diocesan training courses. On one of my fact-finding tours I went to a teachers' training college in one of our leading universities and was allowed to see the two-year course of religious studies in the BEd (Hons) Degree. Only fourteen weeks were given for Sacred writings (A) the Christian Scriptures but nine weeks for the study of (B) non-Christian scriptures. So would-be religious studies teachers who came to the college with only a slender knowledge of the Gospels would leave for the classroom with an inadequate ration of the life and teaching of Jesus to pass on to their young pupils. Little wonder that we have a non-Christian nation! The rest of the college syllabus dealt with the periphery of religion, myth ritual and symbolism, science and religion, religious language, philosophy of religion et alia.

All this gave me an explanation for the ignorance of basic Christian knowledge among even faithful churchgoers and even some clergy. Sermons for some could be for entertainment rather than education.

There are indeed many clever schemes for training church people young and old. Lent courses abound in them but they seem to lack a confident instruction in the basic documents of the Church, the Gospels, which alone can reveal what God has done for us through the earthly life of his Son. I remember a lecture given by Cardinal Daneels of Belgium in my club in London. He said that there were a number of Christian teaching courses which used all modern means of communication but they lacked a call for commitment. It was left for sub-Christian sects to demand this.

So in my search for a solution of modern Christian inertia I at least had discovered the root cause: a steady deposing of the historic Jesus from His place as King and Lord of the universe. To use a modern expression, the Church's situation in England was like 'being up the creek without a paddle'! An Early Father had written, 'Woe to the ship which has no steersman guiding it.' At this point it might be pertinent to ask where were our bishops while all this negative New Testament scholarship was undermining their Church? I can find only one bishop who protested about what was going on. This was Eric Kemp, the Bishop of Chichester. In a debate in the General Synod of the Church of England in 1975 on the subject of the ordination of women to the priesthood, after referring to the gospel records of the words and action of Jesus, he said:

There are two aspects of contemporary theology which create difficulties for us here. The first is that we have and have had for some years now, a strong sceptical school, deriving from Form Criticism and teaching that we can have little certainty about what Our Lord said, did or intended. This seems to me to lead either to a kind of Catholic modernism which says that Christianity rests upon its value in experience but has no historical base or to a view that our only teacher and guide is the Church unchecked by any scripture and free to make what adaptation it thinks right in the circumstance of the day ... Some, even in our own church appear to suggest that the belief in Jesus as true God and true man as hitherto held by the Church is mistaken and some of the issues about the person of Christ which divided Christendom in the fourth and fifth centuries are being reopened. The existence of such confusion in a vital area of belief affecting the authority of the Lord adds to the difficulty of reaching a conclusion about the significance of the Gospel evidence on what Jesus said or did.

In fact, one of our theologians, J. L. Houlden had said that since both Scripture and tradition had lost their authority, all

decisions in church matters must be made simply in the light
of appropriateness and expediency. What more encouragement
did other bishops need to proceed to the ordination of women
to the priesthood? I can find no trace of any support for Eric
Kemp from his fellow bishops, both then and after. So this
new *modus credendi et operandi* has been allowed to govern
religious thinking and teaching at diocesan level!

Yet the aforementioned demise of orthodox New Testament
scholarship has never been the full story. Always within our
Church there has been the theology of men such as C. F. D.
Moule, a Cambridge scholar and others. While I was searching for an answer to the sad state of religious studies I
happened to pick up a paperback, *The Phenomenon Of The
New Testament* by Moule and realised this was a breath of
fresh air. Here I found such statements as, 'The Synoptic
Gospels represent primarily the recognition that a vital
element in evangelism is the plain story of what happened in
the ministry of Jesus' and 'To accept Jesus as Lord without
any historical information would not be about the man Jesus
but only about an ideology or ideal' to which I could add, 'and
this may well describe what passes for churchgoing today'.

Charlie Moule had by then retired to a house on the south
coast, full of years and honours. Although I knew he was an
Evangelical clergyman, on impulse I phoned him at his home
in Pevensey and asked if I could call on him. He replied
quickly and invited me to lunch. A short bird-like figure
covered with an apron and holding a broom, opened the door
and welcomed me like an old friend. We immediately hit it off
and talked while he finished cooking the meal, which I
remember was a very tasty dish of ham cooked in pineapple
juice and vegetables. We started with a delicate glass of sherry
and I felt I was back in a Cambridge college life. He was well
into his eighties but very active, flitting from room to room.
He had nobody to look after him and lived a thoroughly bach-
elor life. He listened to my worries about modern theological
pessimism and dismissed them, calling men like Nineham and
Houlden yesterday's men and really of no account. He was
obviously delighted to be back in a position of tutor and

treated me with great patience. I was keen to get support for an early dating for the Gospels and expressed forthright ideas which he toned down, approaching the problem in a more careful way. I remember he cited St Paul and the Early Church as a proof of the reliability of the Gospels. He invited me to call again and also kept well in touch with a string of letters, most of which I have kept. He still gave seminars to the clergy of the diocese but reported that he was being gradually confined to his house. He then had medical problems and operations until a nephew found a nursing home for him near Sherborne from which he continued to write to me. As I write this he is suffering from arthritis and other alarming symptoms and I am afraid his days may be numbered. However, it has been a stimulating experience sitting at his feet, as it were. I am lucky to have found such a guru.

At the same time I was getting help for my studies from another source. In my visit to the Holy Land I had become very interested in the archaelogical work which was continuing despite the political problems of that troubled land. From the earliest days of the Christian Church pilgrims have not been lacking, for the Holy Places in Jerusalem and Bethlehem and the scenes of out Lord's birth, death and resurrection which have been well celebrated with buildings since the fourth century. Galilee has not aroused such interest and devout Christians have been happy to leave it as a peaceful countryside where Jesus was wont to pray and teach among silent hills. The hymn, 'Dear Lord and Father of Mankind', written in Victorian times, says it all. Scholars have been left to figure out how the Gospels could have been written in such a pastoral setting. However, archaelogists have now turned their attention to Galilee and have found considerable buildings under centuries of neglect. Three major cities have been found which ran across the 'silent hills of Galilee': Caesarea Maritima, Sepphoris, Tiberias. Sepphoris is especially interesting because it is only three or four miles from Nazareth where Jesus spent his young years. It stood in a commanding position overlooking Galilee and had suffered from being caught up in different military actions in both foreign and civil wars shortly before our Lord's time. In 4BC it had become involved in a revolt against foreign rule and taxation and had been ruthlessly destroyed by Varus, the Roman general. However it was too important to be left in ruins and was being rebuilt during Jesus's early years, which leads us to the thought that perhaps he and Joseph were engaged as carpenters and builders in the work there. That it became a fine city (named 'Ornament of Galilee' and 'Pearl of the East') is being revealed as excavations continue. It had many fine houses for successful businessmen of different nationalities, including Jews, and an amphitheatre which could hold five thousand people. Here plays of the great Greek playwrights, Sophocles, Euripides and others would have been performed and possibly Jesus saw them. Certainly his use of the word 'hypocrite' meaning actor is found only in the New Testament part of the Bible.

Generally a picture is emerging of a cosmopolitan Galilee where different languages could be heard, and Hellenistic culture abounded. There was another side to this flourishing Galilean community. To feed this influx of foreigners food had to be grown and supplied by Jewish farmers and this meant sacrificing family smallholdings to larger estates. This put many Jews out of work and forced them into unemployment queues. So a picture of early Jewish daily life shown in the Gospels emerges instead of the later Greek background which some scholars required for their theories of a second generation composition.

As it happened I was becoming excited by the books of Bishop John Robinson, especially *Redating the New Testament* and the *Priority of John* which were being dismissed with tolerant amusement by some Cambridge dons. Then I read a book* by a German archaeologist and papyrologist, Carsten Peter Thiede, who was also an Anglican priest. He claimed he had discovered two small fragments of a gospel, one among the Dead Sea Scrolls which must have been written well

---

* Carsten P. Thiede, *Re-kindling the Word: In Search of Gospel Truth*, Gracewing, 1995.

before AD70 when the monastic community was destroyed by the Romans. Some of Thiede's book is speculative; he nevertheless built a powerful case for a very early date for the Gospels. He quoted a statement by a modern historian that since St Paul gives so few details about the life of the Lord, he must have assumed that his readers could study them for themselves in some written work.

Thiede died recently at the early age of fifty-two but not before he and a team had discovered the real Emmaus which some scholars said did not exist. In a posthumous work he summed up some of his conclusions. In this book, *The Contemporary World of Jesus*, he writes, 'We are piecing together a mosaic. And the test for the reconstruction of events and lives from antiquity can be seen in the ability of a scholar to use all the available evidence to rebuild the structure.' Much of the biblical past still remains to be discovered in sites and manuscripts, but already archaeology is making some New Testament theology outdated. Some ancient dwellings, like the houses of the lower classes, are beyond discovery because they were built of perishable material like mud and rubble but buildings and monuments for the higher classes remain to be discovered if money and experts are available. It has been my good fortune that in retirement I have been able to catch up with these developments. For example I have had time to read Tom Wright's massive work, *Jesus and the Victory of God*.

In this book Wright shows that the setting for Jesus's teaching was the Jewish world which was awaiting the coming of God's kingdom. Parables which have been adopted by other people were addressed in the first place to Jewish society, to the poor as well as to the wealthy. For example the Parable of the Prodigal Son was not originally a general example for life in general but was a call to the Jewish nation to return to God their father from whom they had been separated by their sins. The son represents the Jews who were in exile and the loving father was God who through his Son calls for their return. His first audiences were the lower classes who in great numbers heard him gladly. To a community which was at war with itself Jesus preached love and service. He struck first at the family level and then at a wider public.

In a former book, *According to Luke*, I wrote, 'We need to know how Jesus worked out his special relationship with his Father as he moved among his fellow citizens in a particular country, Palestine, and in a certain age two thousand years ago.' As Moule warned, to accept Jesus without any historical information would not be about the man but about an ideology and goes on to say that we need to know what kind of man Jesus was and how he fitted in with the religious history of Israel.

So what kind of man was he? Here Moule comes to our rescue again. Writing about Luke's theme of the place of women in his Gospel, he says:

> It is difficult enough for any one, even a consummate master of imaginative writing to create a picture of a deeply pure, good person moving about in an impure environment without making him a prig or a prude or a sort of plaster saint. How is it that through all the gospel tradition without exception, there comes a finely-drawn portrait of an attractive young man moving among women of all sorts, including the decidedly disreputable, without a trace of sentimentality, unnaturalness or prudery and yet at every point maintaining a simple integrity of character.

Yet at the same time he was not afraid of being called a winebibber and gluttonous man. He was not afraid also of confronting powerful men in authority with a challenge to the most treasured features of their religion, the Law and Temple. Although all Jews were eagerly awaiting the coming of the kingdom of God which would bring destruction to their enemies and victory for themselves, Jesus turned this theme into another kingdom of love and service and ordered an immediate change of life, a *conversatio morum*, as St Benedict called it five hundred years later.

Jesus went through the towns and villages speaking with a voice of authority which made people sit up and take notice.

He was like a Greek herald, a *kerux* whose duty was to announce news of great importance. To use Tom Wright's illustration Jesus was like somebody driving through a town with a loudhailer 'like a man with a red flag heading off an imminent train disaster'. And disaster was close at hand because the Jews were heading for a confrontation with the powerful Romans which they could never win.

Wright also suggests that Jesus was like a politician on a campaign trail rather than a schoolmaster; more like a composer/conductor than a violin teacher; more like a subversive playwright than an actor. All this helps to show us what kind of man Jesus was and how he related to his people's needs. This is no faded picture of some kind of hero to be placed beside great people of history but the revealer of God's will for his people by his own Son.

So the years of my retirement have been spent trying to piece together the increasing evidence about the composition of the Gospels, rather like putting together a jigsaw just as Thiede suggested, and the search still continues. I feel I can teach and preach the Gospel without any fudge and am no longer like a company chairman who presents an annual report knowing that some of the information is not strictly true. This research has been exciting and I am sorry I have left the classroom to hand it on because I think pupils would find it more exciting than some of the material which passes for religious studies today. However I have been able to write about it and as a result have been asked to speak in parishes, even on the other side of the Atlantic, as I will show in a later chapter.

Chapter Thirteen

Tudor Interlude

I had now reached the age of retirement and although I would have liked to stay on a little longer to establish the pattern of religious studies which I had started, I was getting tired of the daily grind in the classroom which is far more exhausting than people think. The headmaster was also anxious to try the experiment of having a nun as chaplain.

I was brought up to believe that priests never retire but went on until they dropped. This was necessary in the days when there was no pension for the clergy but after the Second World War a scheme was introduced and much later a compulsory age of retirement was fixed beginning at sixty-five or seventy at the latest. It was thought that elderly priests should give way to a younger generation and bring new life to the Church. The trouble was the flow of ordinands was drying up and it became difficult to fill some empty parishes. So began a ministry of retired clergymen. In fact I was never in the position of having to look for further employment because when it was known that I was likely to become available, I received several offers.

I had a letter from the Bishop of Lichfield asking me if I would consider becoming Master of an ancient foundation in Lichfield in the West Midlands. He and I had been at Cambridge together and read the same subjects and he was quite open about the job. It was the Hospital of St John Baptist

Outside the Barrs, founded in 1495 and, far from being anything medical, the Bishop described it as a retirement home for single men over sixty-five. There was a large Master's House with a chapel attached with full Catholic worship to which outside people came. In the Bishop's words it had become a sort of Adullam's cave to which High Churchmen came to get what other parishes did not provide.

It seemed interesting, especially since the Bishop's letter promised free heating and lighting and a small income. So in the autumn of 1981 I went up to Lichfield and met the trustees who were a selection of local inhabitants, together with some members of the Close. They were very friendly and seemed keen for me to accept. So I was conducted round the large premises. The Master's House was basically Tudor and large. It had been brought up to date by the Georgians after which little had been altered. It needed refurbishment because the last master had grown old in it but the chairman of the trustees had said they were planning to spend a lot of money on it – later I discovered that they had a few million pounds in the kitty. My wife came to see it and was horrified at the prospect of having to live in such a large house but was reassured that her wishes would be carried out in any modernisation. In fact we managed to turn it into a very fine building, much admired by all.

So at the end of the Michaelmas term I moved straight into the house in time for Christmas and stayed altogether for ten years. Looking back I think it was a good choice. The last master, Canon Strong, though old was a devout priest and had been respected by all. There was a faithful congregation and well-trained servers so gradually a good church life was built up and an increasing number of worshippers arrived. The residents of the hospital had to attend daily prayers but sometimes had to be prodded, chiefly because I felt they needed to get out of their flats into the fresh air. A daily Mass was possible and a sung Mass on Sundays and feast days. So, you might say, I returned to my origins and had a free hand in church, at any rate.

So far, so good. However, it was not long before feathers

began to be ruffled. The Chairman of the trustees, Leslie Garrett, was a lovely, fatherly man, a local citizen who had made good but remained a gentleman. Others were not so easy; one a local politician who remained a problem for most of my time. It appeared that there was an uneasy relationship between the Bishop and the trustees over who should have responsibility for a new extension of the the hospital in the Close. A few years before I arrived the trustees had helped the diocese with the problem of what to do with the theological college, which had become redundant, opposite the Cathedral. The trustees had stepped in and offered to convert the building into more retirement flats for married couples. The conversion had been paid for out of hospital funds which had been accumulated over the centuries and quite reasonably the trustees insisted that it should some under the care of the Master. The Bishop disagreed and battle was joined which the trustees won. As a result an unhappy situation was set up which surfaced over my appointment. Without the trustees' knowledge the Bishop had sent a letter to me, offering the job with conditions which included free heating and lighting which in such a large house would be considerable. It was one of the reasons I accepted. When the first bills arrived I naturally passed them on to the steward for payment and when it was questioned at the next trustees meeting I produced the Bishop's original letter. They were appalled because they had never seen it and would not have agreed to such a payment. I held my ground but for the sake of peace offered to give up a small part of my annual stipend. So the matter was settled but it left an unpleasant taste which, under a new chairman of trustees, could have become nasty. I was no longer Father Nice Guy who could be manipulated and for the rest of my tenure I was able to retain a certain independence. I was also free from diocesan requirements because the chapel was a 'peculiar' and paid its own way.

Naturally, all this created a chilly relationship with the Close who had sided with their Bishop and I was never invited to preach in the Cathedral, except once on a missionary occasion. A clash with the Dean occurred over a stained-glass window for the hospital chapel which the trustees wished to commission. The Dean had put them in touch with John Piper, the well-known contemporary artist, and a window was commissioned. All this had been done before I became Master and I was a little doubtful about changing the nature of the old chapel which had plain glass and was light and dignified. However the decision had been made and the window neared completion. One afternoon Patrick Rentiens, Piper's partner, brought a cartouche of the design to show some of the trustees. The local paper, the *Lichfield Mercury* was present with a photographer and wanted a picture. Unfortunately the Dean, John Lang, was away and so Patrick and I held up the canvas and this photo appeared in the next edition. John was furious and accused me of stealing his thunder. I told him not to act like a prima donna which did not improve relationships. In due time the final work was fitted and as I suspected changed the appearance of the chapel into a mediaeval place of worship but it was a fine piece of art and has been much admired by the experts. It was, I think, almost John Piper's final work before he died.

Cathedrals with their clergy and wives in a close seem to breed a special form of life, almost a holier-than-thou atmosphere into which one enters with a sense of privilege and almost reverence. The Cathedral itself was an historic building which at one time was the centre of the vast kingdom of Mercia which once stretched from the Midlands to the border of Cumbria. Its great missionary bishop was St Chad whose bones were buried in Lichfield and in the twelfth century were reverenced by pilgrims from a wide area. For this lodgings (hospitals or places of hospitality) were needed and this is how my Hospital of St John Baptist outside the walls or barrs came to be founded by Augustinian monks in AD 1123. It is still possible to open a door in the present vestry and descend into the original foundations. This, of course, has made the whole building a place of historical interest.

In more modern times new centres of population and industry, like Birmingham, Manchester and Liverpool have been carved out of the original kingdom, isolating Lichfield and its

Cathedral and making then places which time has passed by. As a result a provincial life has been created, the sort of place which writers like Flaubert in France, Chekhov in Russia and George Eliot in England used for their works. I did not realise this at the time but now on reflection begin to understand the new kind of society in which I found myself. Here local successes and triumphs gave as much satisfaction as wider achievements. For example, there were several upmarket local committees and a sign that you had advanced socially was when you were elected to serve on one. Such was the council or trustees of my hospital which was reckoned to be of little account until it became known that its resources could be counted in millions. Suddenly there was no shortage of aspirants! I had to watch that my position of Master was not overwhelmed by local personalities making their mark.

It was a new experience for me because although I had been used to small communities in the course of my life they had not been so encapsulated. Moreover, I was still on the edge of the Church of England because St John's chapel was a 'peculiar', in other words it was outside diocesan organisation and I was not bothered by things like quotas. But I was accepted into the local community, invited to become a Rotarian, to teach Latin at the college of further education, to be chaplain to the Mayor and to take part in many other activities. But at last I had space to catch up with my theological reading and to begin writing again. Because I have always believed the Gospels were written early rather than late I welcomed John Robinson's books, especially *The Priority of John* and because I suspected it would not have a wide readership prepared a more simple version which I called, *Another Look at St John's Gospel*. This took off slowly but eventually sold out.

I also renewed my contact with Cambridge, joining the Cambridge Society and becoming a long-serving member of the executive committee. As I wrote earlier I returned to Sri Lanka to extend its work more widely. I was also invited to lead more pilgrimages to the Holy Land and so kept in touch with all the archaelogical discoveries there, chiefly in Galilee. All these occupations were centred on my beautiful Tudor house in Lichfield which had been restored regardless of expense by the trustees and had become a very desirable residence, much envied by my friends but not entirely accepted by my wife who longed for a proper retirement in Cornwall. In the end, after ten years, I gave way and finally retired at seventy-five although I still had a lot of life in me to help those Catholic churchpeople who were struggling to keep afloat in alien seas.

My ten years at Lichfield also gave me further information about what was happening to religious studies in state schools where there was still a strong requirement for Christian education. My recent experience had been in the private sector where I had a free hand to plan my own curriculum as I have already described. Now I found myself in close contact with state schools. There were two large comprehensive schools in Lichfield, one of which traced its origin to the grammar school attended by the great Dr Johnson, opposite St John's Hospital. Once a year we had an old boys' commemoration in my chapel. The headmaster of the other large school was one of my regular communicants, so I was welcomed in both and had a chance to learn what was going on in religious education. It soon became apparent that little was being taught about the historic Jesus and that was to be expected when I learnt that the diocesan education programmes suffered from the same defect. My daughter was teaching in a primary school where there also was a minimum Christian content. Sometimes she would ask me for advice about a church festival and when I replied she would say, 'I cannot teach that because it is too Christian and that might offend other religions.' It was interesting that neither I nor another priest who had spent some years teaching in a classroom were invited to be on the diocesan education commitee. The priest who was director of religious education had no classroom experience.

If the diocese did not want to use my teaching experience the secular county education authority did, and I was invited to give a lecture to a large audience of teachers of religious studies. I expounded on how I had planned my syllabus round the first three Gospels and how my pupils had become very involved. At the end of my talk one teacher said, 'I didn't realise we could give such Christian lessons,' and many others nodded their heads in agreement.

I even went back to the classroom for a term. My old school at Wellingborough was only a shortish distance away and suddenly lost its chaplain. So once a week I drove down and taught mainly the fifth form which was co-educational; my first experience of mixed classes and which needed special handling. I found the all-too familiar lack of Christian text books and instead, a course on the Hindu religion. So for a term I did my best to set the classes on a gospel course.

I mentioned earlier that I had been asked to teach Latin at the local college of Further Education. A Rotarian colleague, Ian James, was the principle and had applicants for this subject. I was surprised to find such a need but took it on and found that over nearly ten years I was never short of pupils, some of whom showed great ability, gaining O levels. This led on to another course on St John's Gospel which attracted a wide audience of good solid Brummies and which provided material for my first book, *Another Look at St John's Gospel*. At the same time, I was chairman of the diocesan Church Union which was still the main High Church society. It became clear that modern churchpeople had little knowledge of this great movement and I realised that I should attempt an up-to-date history when I finally retired.

Chapter Fourteen

Retirement Deferred

As my wife and I drove through the gates of the Master's House for the last time I reflected that for once I had no new challenge to face except perhaps how to occupy my free time. There was, of course, a new book to finish with a certain amount of research but no pastoral work. We had bought a house in the Cornish fishing village of Looe with a fine view over the river and near my old parish of Lanteglos-by-Fowey. I then heard that its vicar had suddenly taken off for a chaplaincy overseas and a locum was needed while a new incumbent was found. I was asked by the rural dean to take it on for the time being and so I found myself again among my old parishioners who by now had grown up considerably: after all I had been away for twenty-five years. It was great fun working with those I had baptised and prepared for Confirmation. It was on my last Sunday, which was Easter Day, that an unfortunate incident happened. The lovely old parish church which stood in the countryside beside a farm was packed for our Sung Mass which I celebrated with a another retired priest assisting me. When we came to the Communion I drank first from the chalice and felt a burning in my mouth. I passed it over to my assistant who had the same feeling. I said, 'We cannot give this to the congregation' and carried the chalice out of the church and poured its contents on the ground. I returned and consecrated fresh wine using a fresh cruet of water. All was well, I finished Mass with little delay and the congregation went away happy. It was time to discover why the wine was tainted. There was no running water in the church and a bottle was brought up from the village the night before and put in a cupboard. It so happened that there was another bottle there containing a colourless spirit used for removing candle wax and the churchwarden had used this when preparing the Mass cruets. I had only taken a small sip but my mouth burned for days afterward. Over the years I had celebrated Mass in all sorts of conditions but this was something new! The churchwarden was covered with confusion and the poor man died within the year: not I hope because of shame.

It was 1992 and I had been retired a year. I was nearing the end of my book, *Marginal Catholics*, which was proving larger than I had expected. I went to Oxford to complete my research and was there on my birthday, 11 November, when the blow came. I switched on my radio and heard the announcement that the General Synod had voted for women priests by one vote. For a number of years this issue had been debated but it was thought that it could still be defeated, especially since women had been brought into the diaconate a few years earlier. It seemed that the new Archbishop of Canterbury, George Carey, had put his job on the line and a woman of Catholic persuasion had changed sides at the last moment. There is no doubt that the Catholic Group was politically naive and had lost the expertise it once had at the time of the Anglican/Methodist controversy. Surely on such a crucial matter as a change in the traditional ministry a two-thirds majority should have been demanded by the Catholic party! But a false optimism seemed to have prevailed and therefore too little preparation had been made if the vote went the wrong way. An organisation called Cost of Conscience was being formed but was still in its early stage and was in no position to deal with the chaos resulting from so great a change in ministry. Just as in the game of snooker a player may drive the cue ball in to an ordered pattern of balls and send them in all directions, this happened to traditional and devout church people who went off in many directions.

This had happened in North America ten years earlier when a few maverick bishops illegally ordained some women and the official Church, the Episcopal Church of the USA (ECUSA) followed suit. Some traditional bishops and clergy left the Established Church and set up independent dioceses. This has posed problems in such a vast country where communication can be difficult and both church buildings and finance have to be found. When a long-established structure begins to fall apart, it is never easy to put the pieces together again like Humpty Dumpty. So it is still proving difficult to set up a satisfactory orthodox and united rival church. Personalities and cultural backgrounds once held together by a central authority begin to provide problems once they become independent. In Britain it is different of course because we are a small country, but differences of churchmanship and other material problems have to be solved before orthodox Anglicans can settle down within their own integrity.

In 1992 the Church of England had all these difficulties in front of them but in my retired state I could only sit back and watch it trying to get out of the situation it had caused. Meanwhile out the blue I received an invitation from a man who had been in my youth club at the beginning of the war to go to Canada and preach at his ordination in the traditional Anglican Catholic Church. Jimmy Corps had retired with his wife Hetty, also in the same youth club, after a good job in insurance and was living on Vancouver Island. As far as I could understand he had become involved with the traditional Church which had broken away from the official Church of Canada when it had followed the American example of ordaining women. I knew little then about what was happening on the other side of the Atlantic but since my fare would be paid I thought I should accept the invitation. The idea was that I should fly to Ottawa first and stay for a few days with Bishop Robert Mercer who had come from Matabeleland to take over the further organisation of the young traditional church.

So toward the end of March and also of Lent I flew into a snow-covered Ottawa and was met by the Bishop and driven to his small flat in the city. He was a monk of the Community of the Resurrection at Mirfield and lived simply, relying for financial support from local church people. I had not been warned about the cold but fortunately wore a leather coat which mostly kept out the still-cold weather. Since I knew little about the church situation in Canada the Bishop gave a short run-down of the situation. It seemed that when the official Canadian Episcopal Church followed America in ordaining women, some Anglican priests left their Church and went independent. One was an outstanding Ottawa vicar, Father Camino de Catanzaro who on one Sunday led his congregation out of their parish church and held services in a local school. Under his leadership the Traditional Church began to spread throughout Canada: Fr de Cat was reluctantly consecrated bishop and with the help of a Cowley father, Roland Palmer, SSJE, built up a framework of sound teaching and liturgy. The new bishop threw himself into his work with such vigour that his health suffered and he died. His widow, Joan, takes up the story:

> The three years which remained in the life of the newly-consecrated bishop were full of travelling and organising of parishes and the diocese which stretched from sea to sea . . . He had no secretarial help, no immediate funds, only the loyalty and faithfulness to Christ and his Church of knowledgeable, traditional Anglicans. It would take many years to rebuild the Church which had been eroded by modernism and apathy for a long time.

When Bishop de Cat, as he was affectionately known, died there was no natural successor. However a priest in his seventies, Dr Alfred Woolcock of the parish of the Good Shepherd Oshawa, was elected as a stopgap until a younger man could be found. Then to the rescue came Robert Mercer from South Africa and it was he who sheltered with me from the cold and briefed me about the sad state of religion in North America and the threat of extreme feminism. He introduced me to a book by Donna Steichen, *Ungodly Rage,* which was a well-documented account of how the nature of God was being challenged. I also read how this was infiltrating the parishes. One Vancouver parish was using Lenten devotions addressed to Woman God.

It was the week before Holy Week and on 25 March we celebrated the feast of the Annunciation in the small cathedral which had been brought from a redundant Pentecostal group. The Dean was a retired civil servant, his assistant priests earned their living in secular jobs, the congregation was generous with their money and was growing to such an extent that expansion was being planned. After Mass the Bishop thought we should have a bit of luxury and we had a delicious meal in a creperie. Ottawa was full of restaurants of every kind and nationality. In the afternoon Joan de Catanzaro, the bishop's widow, drove me to the edge of the arctic wastes. On Palm Sunday I preached at the Solemn Mass where the ceremonial was dignified and the rite traditional. Many of the congregation were refugees from modern liberal liturgies. One evening I was able to address members of the Ottawa branch of the Cambridge Society and answer their questions about what was happening in our university.

After nearly a week I flew into the slightly warmer climate of Vancouver in the west and then transferred to a small plane which skimmed over the water to Vancouver Island. Some local passengers were joking and said, 'Don't ask when we will arrive but if!' All was well and I was met at the small airport by Jim and Hetty and taken to their lovely home beside the water. Neither had changed very much since the Lamorbey days. After serving with the RAF Jim had emigrated with his wife and Canadian in-laws and landed a good job with a Vancouver insurance company. The family were good church people and had joined those who left the liberal official Anglican Church and joined the Traditional Church. This was spreading throughout Canada but did not make the mistake of ordaining men to the priesthood without proper training. In such a vast country another bishop was needed for the west. Fortunately the dean of the official cathedral in Victoria had changed sides and retired to Ladysmith, round the corner from Jim and Hetty. This was Bob Crawley, a Yorkshireman who

built up a successful business in Canada, then left to train for
the priesthood. This was in the years before the controversial
ordination of women. Now he was just the man to take charge
of traditionalists in western Canada and was elected bishop in
1986. By then he was in his middle sixties, an age when most
English bishops were retiring. But he had plenty of energy left
and continued into the next century. Jim became his secretary,
then a deacon and was encouraged to study for the priesthood.
Now this was about to happen and I had been invited to take
part in his ordination, just after Easter. Meanwhile I became
great friends with Bishop Bob Crawley, a small round man
with a great sense of humour and of many accomplishments,
including hunting wild animals of which there is an abundance
in British Columbia. He took me on several expeditions into
the pine forests where the bear and cougar roam. He would
call for me with a gun under his arm then we walked into the
forest, looking for cougars. I am sorry I cannot say we met
any but it was reported that one rampaged through a local
hotel, causing havoc. However Bob would keep up a running
commentary on the religious scene and how priests and lay
people out of frustration with poor theology and worship in
the established Church of Canada were either leaving it or
joining the Traditional Church. One lady said to me, 'Our
religion had become man-centred rather than God centred.'
The Bishop was a mine of information about first pioneers in
Canada who in the absence of any missionaries would meet in
small groups in log cabins and read morning and evening
prayer together. He himself had known what it was like to live
in isolated areas of the North with little amenities – a tough
man indeed. There was no proper church in Ladysmith and
both the Bishop and Jim had made small chapels in their
homes where small congregations would gather.

   Jim's ordination was held in St John's Church in Victoria
which had been bought for the ACCC (Anglican Catholic
Church of Canada) which had become the name of the Traditional Church a few years earlier. Before that they had
worshipped in private houses. The church was beautifully
equipped with the Reservation of the Blessed Sacrament, a

statue of our Lady of Walsingham amongst other furnishings. The vicar was Father Peter Wilkinson, an unmarried priest who earned his living as a clerk in the legal department of the local government. The ordination Mass at which I preached was perfectly celebrated and afterwards the large congregation was handsomely entertained.

The next day I returned to Victoria to give a talk on the state of religion in Britain to a wider audience. I was unsparing in my criticism of what was happening in the Church of England and how church life was being undermined by radical New Testament theology. My talk was reported and brought an attack in the main daily newspaper by a clergyman of the official Church – a follower of the notorious liberal Bishop Spong, it transpired – who said I had got it all wrong and everything in his part of the vineyard was lovely. It appeared this was not the general view and I had a letter from one of the Cathedral staff apologising for the attack and indicating that all were not happy with what was happening in the official Church of Canada.

I returned to England with much food for thought but first had to endure the long flight. The plane was packed and I was uncomfortably seated. However I had a piece of luck. A stewardess had put my heavy bag in the locker above me but had not shut it properly and it fell on my head, stunning me momentarily. The stewardess was alarmed and escorted me to the first-class cabin where I was given splendid treatment. Next to me was an elderly lady, well made-up and elegantly clothed in black. I was dressed as a priest and after a while we chatted about our lives. It soon became clear that she was a madam in a brothel in Vancouver but the conversation flowed and I was not certain whether she wanted absolution or was sizing me up as possible client in her London branch! After a gourmet lunch with wine we fell silent and I was left to my thoughts about what I experienced in the Church in Canada. It was clear that I had been given a close look at what happened when a structure fell apart and a smaller part was left to fend for itself; no income, no buildings, no status. How would similar orthodox clergy and laity fare at home?

I was invited back the next year to give two lectures on new developments in biblical theology to the annual General Synod of the whole ACCC which was going to be held on Vancouver Island in Victoria University. I was reluctant to face the long flight again but finally was persuaded because my expenses would be paid and I would be able to stay with my friends, Jim and Hetty. Jim was secretary of the Synod. So in the late spring I flew out and was very glad I did because the Synod was an inspiration for one who had spent many years in the tired old Church of England at home. There were nearly a hundred delegates from all over Canada and this meant a long and expensive journey for some who had to travel from the east to the west coast, paying their own fares and accommodation. A number were young and enthusiastic, full of ideas for the growth of their Church and united despite differences of churchmanship. Robert Mercer presided and we had with us Archbishop Falk who was the Metropolitan of the growing worldwide Traditional Church. In the next few years I was to have further dealings with him until he just vanished into thin air. A strange man.

I gave two lectures on 'The Fading Out and The Recovery of the Historic Jesus' and was surprised to discover how ignorant of the Scriptures were most of my audience. Bishop Mercer had to confess that he had been guilty of accepting liberal theories about the Gospels.

From Archbishop Falk I learnt that there were attempts to set up the Traditional Church in England and the name of Father Whiting was mentioned. So on my return I contacted him and was given a list of interested people in the south-west, one of whom was my former commander at Culdrose, now retired. Another was a retired colonel, David Rogers, who was an officer of the Prayer Book Society. I was still living in Cornwall and helped to organise a new branch of the Traditional Anglican Church, the TAC. For some churchpeople it was the only retreat from the Established Church which had voted for women priests and we soon had a number of followers who were also refugees from modern liturgies. The 1662 Book of Common Prayer for them became a standard around which mostly conservative churchmen could rally. This was certainly not my cup of tea but I hoped I could lead them into broader ways of worship. There was really no other way because the Catholic party was only slowly organising what would be called Forward In Faith which infiltrated only slowly from cities and towns to the countryside. However it soon became clear to me that there was no future in England for a traditional party which was backward-looking and appealed chiefly to the older generation. There was too great eagerness to have its own bishops and priests before they had any growth. There was an attempt to make me a bishop instead of Whiting but I made it clear that until we had a programme of teaching and training I was not interested. So a small caucus elected Whiting and he was consecrated in a hotel in Fareham by three imported bishops.

By then I had decided to offer my help to Forward In Faith which was growing round the country and was invited to join the central council so that I might forge a link with disenchanted members of the TAC which was making few converts.

Earlier, I said the vote for women priests had sent some Anglo-Catholics off in all directions. This was especially true of many clergy, most of whom went over to Rome and were retrained at the Roman Catholic seminary at Wonersh. Some Roman Catholic dioceses welcomed them for they were experiencing a shortage of priests and quickly found posts for them, even with their families. For example in my home parish of Looe, the Roman parish priest who serves both the Carmelite monastery and local Catholics was once a curate in a Plymouth Anglican parish and he still has his wife and children with him!

This left some notable Anglo-Catholic parishes without a vicar and retired priests like myself were asked to help. As a former secretary of the Church Union I was especially in demand when some difficult situation arose. Diocesan bishops were not always sensitive to the needs of those of another integrity and might even use underhand methods to infiltrate women priests into parishes who had voted against them. The consecration of 'flying bishops' went some way toward solving this problem but sometimes they were helpless, especially when a diocesan bishop resented an intrusion into his area.

All this was more complicated because there was a great ignorance both of the Faith and also of our Catholic inheritance: Keble, Pusey and Newman meant little to most churchpeople. It was for them that I wrote my first long book, *Marginal Catholics*. Perhaps even more alarming was a general ignorance of the Bible, even of the Gospels and so when I was invited to give talks in parishes I insisted on gospel study and wrote a simple commentary on St Luke's Gospel.

It had not escaped my memory the conclusion of Nineham and Houlden in the 1970s that since it was not possible to discover from the Gospels what Jesus has actually taught we had to rely on convenience and appropriateness for making religious policy and decisions. Since many of our top churchmen would have been taught by these radical scholars, it was not difficult to understand why they could promote and support a priesthood of women. The appointment of twelve men as the basis of future ministry by our Lord at the Last Supper was clearly recorded in the Gospels – 'he came with the Twelve' – and the Catholic Church had faithfully followed his command and survived social changes through the ages. Now in the twentieth century the Anglican Church was prepared to overrule our Lord's provision for his Church because of the changed status of women. In the absence of sufficient knowledge about recent orthodox New Testament scholarship, the battle for women priests and bishops had been fought by both parties on different ground.

All this I was beginning to understand but appeared to be a pelican in the wilderness because it seemed nobody was willing to listen to an ageing and retired priest to whom it was becoming clear that new evidence was showing the Gospels were written early rather than later and were quickly carried round the civilised countries of the Roman Empire. So in the words of the hymn, 'We have a gospel to proclaim' as long as I am able, in writing and speaking, I am trying to bring back the historic Christ into the life of the Church.

All this has meant a lot of travelling which I could not do from Cornwall so having made provision for my family I moved closer to London living wherever I would find a space and looking after myself.

My friend, David Rogers, let me have a small house on his property near Salisbury and here I stayed for several years doing what I could to help those who were troubled by the continuing debate over women priests. It seemed to me that there was an urgent need for a manual on sound teaching because the training which priests and lay readers were getting from the diocese was flawed since it followed too closely the liberal scholarship of those who were already 'yesterday's men' as one prominent theologian told me. For example Nineham's commentary on St Mark, published cheaply in a Pelican series, had not been updated and was readily available for students. My experience in Canada showed that some guide through contemporary scholarship was needed. So I settled down to write another book which I called *A Church in Miniature*. It included the rough commentary on the first three Gospels which I prepared for my fifth form at Roedean. It was published by Gracewing in 1996 but sold very slowly.

Although I was slowing up I managed to lead another pilgrimage to the Holy Land and saw the progress being made on excavations in Galilee. David then became ill and I did my best to nurse him until just before his death. I then was asked to help in the parish where I was brought up many years ago, St Barnabas, Beckenham and here I learnt how difficult it was to keep a church alive in a modern suburban parish which had become a dormitory for London workers. However, it was a plesant way to round off my priestly career especially when there were members of the congregation who remembered me when I was first ordained.

I was now in my eighties and looked around for a place to end my days without becoming a burden on my family. Fortunately I was offered a flat in a college for retired clergy where body and soul were cared for and I could go quietly into the next world . . . It was not to be . . . one afternoon during my after lunch rest, a college tradition, my phone rang and an American voice announced itself as Bishop Sigillito and asked if he could come down to discuss one of my books. So, one day he came down to Lingfield in a taxi – he never travelled any other way in this country – and we began an association which is still continuing. He was very interested in *A Church In Miniature* and my positive suggestions for the future of the Church. He was a stockily-built man in his early fifties and full of energy. He had been elected bishop recently for a traditional church in St Louis. He was also an international lawyer and flew to Britain regularly on business which seemed very profitable. He was anxious to establish my book as a manual for his people, many of whom were discontented Roman Catholics and Anglicans. As I wrote earlier I had heard how women priests and bishops and an increasing liberal theology in the official church (ECUSA) had sent members flying in all directions but had little idea about the subsequent chaos. Bishop Martin put me in the picture about attempts to create an orthodox united Anglican Church but again as I noted before, once a single structure is broken up it is never easy to create another one. The Bishop also described the troubles within the Roman Catholic Church over paedophile cases which caused such anger that in some parts of the States priests could no longer appear in clerical dress in public. Here, too, liberal teaching and worship were driving people out. He had been brought up as a Roman Catholic but had left over the scandals and had joined traditional Anglicans in St Louis. His academic learning made him a sure cert for leadership there and he was also making his influence felt among other bishops, inside and outside the official Church.

He next invited me to give a series of lectures to his people in St Louis and possibly to others as well. I was now well into my eighties and was not keen to make such a long trip but I had never been to the States and my fare would be paid. The Bishop also promised I would be looked after at the airports and so just before Holy Week I went on yet another adventure. It was not a very comfortable flight and I had a long wait at New Jersey airport during which I was nearly swept with a crowd of Chinese into a plane bound for Hong Kong but I finally made the shorter flight to St Louis where I was met by the Bishop and his right-hand man, Don, who was of Japanese origin. We quickly drove round the edge of the city to the Bishop's house and I was able to take in the general scene which I seemed to have seen before on American films. The Bishop's family of three children: two boys and a girl all under sixteen also seemed familiar from the same source. His wife was also a lawyer and was away all day so he did the cooking and even the laundry. 'When did your bishop at home ever wash your clothes?' he asked me as he handed me clean pants and vest, and I had to reply that it was not a normal episcopal duty at home! He cooked well in mostly Italian style, not surprising since his family were of that origin. In fact, most of the people I met were of varied ethnic stock but now were completely Americanised.

Mostly we ate in expensive clubs and excellent restaurants and I was never hungry. I was also fully engaged in speaking – eight lectures on my St Luke book and three on the *Church In Miniature*. On one occasion I had five bishops in my audience. All this had to be fitted into Holy Week and Easter services which were held in a rented Presbyterian church building and shared with Korean Methodists. Like most traditional churches the bishop's flock had no building of their own but were saving up for their own place.

There was no service on Good Friday and one of the congregation took me to the ceremonies in the old Episcopal church which were well carried out and attended. It seemed just like home until it was pointed out that some of the clergy might have been ordained by a woman bishop – a warning for the future in Britain. The Bishop's wife had remained a Roman Catholic but found the local church so liberal in its faith and worship that she and the children would come to her husband's Mass which, though simple, was devoutly celebrated. There were other priests on the Bishop's staff, all earning their living in other professions, one an optician, another a carpenter and yet another a bishop who was a retired doctor. The whole set-up seemed almost amateur but it worked and an increasing number of people seemed grateful for sound teaching and worship.

During my stay the Bishop appointed me his canon theologian and that gave me a foot on orthodox ground if all failed at home. So I returned home having made many friends who kept in touch with me and I sit back wondering, 'What next?'

Chapter Fifteen

Concerning Spiritual Matters

After I finished writing this book I had time to ask myself the question, 'How did my religious life stand up to such continual movement?' There were times when I had to operate as a priest without a fixed church or chapel; sometimes it was difficult to find a quiet place where I could say my prayers and read my daily office. Yet somehow I have managed to survive with my faith intact. The answer can probably be found in my early upbringing and training. If, as the Jesuits are reputed to say, the first six years of a child's life are vital for commitment in later years then I had three times that amount of years for the consolidation and development of the spiritual life.

From the age of two I was taken by my parents to the weekly High Mass at our parish church. Only once did I misbehave myself by kicking the pew in front for which I was so soundly told off that I never did it again. In fact I was entirely absorbed by the ceremonial and when I was six I was called out of the pew to take part in it as a boat boy. After that I rose steadily to take more responsible parts in the Liturgy. The years after the First World War were exciting for the Oxford or High Church movement. Opposition from other parts of the Church of England had been blunted by the heroic lives of devoted parish priests who faced all kinds of hardship to bring back the Catholic faith into their Church and now Anglo-Catholics went on the attack with successful Congresses and other celebrations. It was an exciting time for a growing boy who had been given sound teaching and no doubt it was the reason why the seeds of a priestly vocation were sown in his mind. I was introduced early to some of the great spiritual writers like St Francis de Sales and St John of the Cross who taught me the first stages of meditation. In those days there were no rival entertainments like television and so there was plenty of time for reading. I was also given a glimpse of monastic life when I was taken to serve at a community of nuns at Haywards Heath. Many years later I became their confessor at Rempstone. I, early in life, learnt about the love of God and devotion to the sacred heart of Jesus which I have never lost.

All this was contained within the Church's year beginning with the sombre four weeks of Advent followed by the excitement of Christmas which never began before Christmas Eve. Lent was always kept with some austerity, even in my very young days. Easter was celebrated literally with trumpets and drums and fine music in contrast to the unaccompanied Palestrina of the previous forty days. A whole crop of festivals kept us all on our toes until Advent came again. Altogether a solid programme of faith and practice filled my days and equipped me for any challenges which might follow.

And of course they did follow suddenly with the outbreak of war and the discovery in the Army that very few had any beliefs at all. As I look back at those bleak years I marvel at the way I was able to adapt my early religious experience to such conditions and to the minimal Anglican churchmanship which a Protestant chaplaincy department allowed us. It was still the Mass which mattered and it could be celebrated in a bare garrison church or from the tailboard of an army lorry. So my faith stood firm until I could emerge into brighter days. Even then my way back was slow via simple public school religion and naval life to an Anglo-Catholic parish in Cornwall. Since then my life has been thoroughly occupied in teaching people how to adapt to changes in the Church and to a diminishing church attendance.

From time to time the Roman Catholic Church has beckoned me but I have never been seriously tempted possibly because of my Anglo-Catholic upbringing and also because I have always been kept busy trying to keep my present Church on a steady course. Even when that Church has surrendered part of its Catholic heritage, I have found refuge in traditional churches and have been able to feed them with sound teaching material. The more I see what is going on in the Roman Church, the more I feel there is no safe haven in this life. Meanwhile I try to comfort the faithful remnant in my own church and feel I must remain with them unless the situation becomes impossible. Perhaps I am like a naval embarkation officer evacuating troops from a hopeless situation and being the last to leave.

It would be remiss if I ended without writing about the considerable influence of the monastic life on my continuing struggle in the spiritual combat. While at Cambridge I was helped by the Cowley Fathers and learnt to make retreats in their London house. Then more than forty years ago I was accepted as an oblate at the Benedictine Abbey at Nashdom (later Elmore) and came under the care of the abbot, Dom Augustine Morris who until his death a few years ago was like a father to me. Religious communities in the Anglican Church have had a difficult time in recent years, not least because of a decline in the number of vocations but somehow they manage to survive and to remain a challenge and example to a mainly godless country. They also provide a haven of peace and silence for those seeking a respite from a noisy daily life. No evidence in the spiritual life can be made without times of silence and these I continue to treasure.

Anglican Benedictines in recent years have had to fight hard to distance themselves from the controversies of the secular church and have not always been successful but it is useful to remember that the Benedictine life is worldwide and transcends denominational boundaries. Above all it provides a regular system of prayer in the full Daily Office which keeps our minds directed towards God at fixed times in the day. I have used it throughout most of my life and find it a great consolation in old age. In the words of the Psalmist I can cry regularly, 'Forsake me not when I am old and greyheaded . . .'

Chapter Sixteen

Final Score

A short time ago I was asked to preach for an unusual occasion. My oldest friend, Arthur Fincham, now ninety-seven, was celebrating ninety years of serving at the altar. I had just passed ninety and so our association was a long one. We had both been brought up in St George's Church, Beckenham, a large church with an impressive sanctuary and seven years later I also took my place as a server, boat boy. Both had remained faithful church members, I as a priest and Arthur as a top accountant. In my sermon at the celebration Mass I asked what had kept us faithful over the years and suggested that it was the training we had received in those early years which had proved an unshakeable foundation. To take part in rich ceremonial in an impressive sanctuary was an awesome experience. The presence of a mighty God seemed overpowering but it was supported by sound Christian revelation in the weekly Sunday school where the Gospels were distilled into a small boy's mind, illustrated with a series of stamps, I seem to remember.

Those were the days before modern scholarship had muddied the clear waters of the gospel stories. The unfathomable greatness of the God we both worshipped was matched by the teaching of His Son, Jesus Christ. In those days of Anglo-Catholic progress between the wars great mission priests, often monks, filled our churches with sermons which called for deep commitment, almost like Salvation Army preachers. All this impressed young men and women and helped some of them through the dark years of the Second World War.

Now in my niney-first year I can look back with gratitude at those early years which were not shared by many of my contemporaries and indeed by the counrty at large. My own parish church might have been well-filled but many were struggling and the result was a mainly unbelieving nation which sent a whole generation of young people uninstructed in the Christian faith into a dangerous world. Early in this book I showed how I had come face to face with this unbelief which even in darkest days made combatants unable to meet the last enemy, death, even when a priest was at hand to prepare them for this final event.

I suppose this was a shaking experience which challenged the religious foundation of my early years and there was no escape from it and I was left to make the best of a bad job. I shall never forget my first attempt to teach a hut full of soldiers Christian belief and being shouted down in the process. Nor will I forget sharing a gunnery position under fierce German fire with fellow members of my regiment in the Appenines in the Italian campaign in 1944. Sheer animal fear was in their eyes yet they were unable to ask for help from their priest who also was a casualty but stayed to continue ministration to any who might need it.

All this was hard for a young priest of twenty-six who had joined the Army with high hopes of being needed in battle but was left in no doubt that the Church's task after the war would not be an easy one. This to some extent made me different from many of my fellow priests who had not been face to face with sheer unbelief. I think my call for a much deeper basic training has not really been answered in the parish teaching programmes which appear regularly. In fact unbelief in this country and in other countries of the west has reached a point of no return and we are left to fight modern struggles for survival without understanding what the Christian faith has to offer. Hidden beneath all systems of teaching the Christian faith is the underlying command by Jesus to love; to love God but also our neighbours. To express it like that may seem too sentimental an approach and yet it is a sober fact that we have never managed to put it into practice and therefore remain unloving and unloveable. Love has been defined as doing the best for the other despite the cost and mostly we fail but where this has been applied in daily life people can live happily together. St Benedict put this command at the centre of his Holy Rule for monasteries and was able to create communities out of refugees fleeing from the fall of Rome 500 years after Christ. Brethren should love and respect their fellow monks and thus follow Jesus's teaching as he preached first to families in Galilee. A loving relationship between men and women under the eye of God was meant to bring peace everywhere but it has not happened. There has been much love but God has been left out and it has become horribly wrong, as a glance at our daily papers will show much sex, little love. Where true love is found sheer delight follows and God is glorified. A prayer in the Daily Office sums up what is needed:

Lord our God, makes us love you above all things,
and all our fellowmen with a love that is worthy of you.

Some people find it difficult to love but I have always found it easy to love those around me, probably because I was surrounded by love in my family. My father always had a rapport with all he had dealings with and I seem to have inherited it. Also I was taught early the art of meditation, seeking God in prayer which can lead to understanding his love for me and although it has often been crowded out of my life I can still use silence to renew my searching. Love can sometimes help me have empathy with others and this is a deeper thing than sympathy because it has allowed me to enter into another's feelings – as I said earlier in this book it is invaluable for a teacher. If love can come easily it can get out of hand in relationships with others and has to be disciplined. As I look back in my life I have to confess that I have sometimes failed but mostly in loving and caring too much for another. Love can be a great healer but this can be a risky business! Absence of love and respect can threaten a community and lead to crime and war where the only alternative is law and punishment. At present in our country we are faced with dangers within and attack from outside, our prisons are full and our armies engaged abroad. How long can our planet survive such conditions?

If this wasn't enough, we have the threat of global warming which may well make our planet uninhabitable because of intense heat. Our world which we have always thought ever-lasting has suddenly looked very vulnerable and may well share the fate of other planets in the universe which have disappeared. It is interesting to read our Lord's predictions in the Gospels about the end of all things: seas out of control, the heavens shaken, portents appearing in the skies. Is it possible that events announced in that difficult book, the Apocalypse, may soon happen? Will then our Lord appear and give his judgement on a world which ignored his teaching of love?

Reaching ninety was a shock. Earlier decades had slipped past almost unnoticed because there was space for new experiences and to plan for the future. In my seventies I visited Canada for the first time to give some lectures and in my eighties I again crossed the Atlantic and had my first sight of the States for the same reason and received a canonry, somehing I had never attained in my own country. But ninety! It seems like a dead end and planning for the future must be strictly limited. There may be yet some years ahead as my friend Arthur is having but warning signs appear and it is better not to take interest in future events. Why worry about results in the Olympic Games in 2012 or regaining the Ashes in 2008? It is too much to hope for a view from another shore. Life in fact can be like a long distance race, a marathon perhaps. You start off with many friends beside you but one by one they drop out until you are almost alone. At my last college event only one of my year had survived.

Doctors say I am still reasonably healthy with good blood pressure and other parts still working except my ears which were deafened by guns in battle – my war wound. It is amazing that my memory is good, even of early events of my life, and this has helped me write this last book. 'Lord, let me know my end and the number of my days' cried the Psalmist but the good Lord tends to be silent on this matter and this is the story of my whole life. A master at my school used to repeat the adage, 'Man proposes, God disposes'. It may have been noticed that my life has taken a number of unexpected turns. I started out intending to be a good parish priest but instead have ended up a soldier, naval officer, administrator, teacher, and finally author – and none of my own making.

As I look round I see so may things essential for the welfare and safety of God's creation are disappearing: love, peace, education and finally a healthy environment, that I feel we have reached a point of no return. How long can this state of affairs continue or is the end of all things really at hand? If so will I survive long enough to share the fate of all mankind, a suitable ending for a pelican in the wilderness?

Appendix

What about the Infrastructure?

A Sermon Preached by Fr Ivan Clutterbuck

A valley of decision

Problems come at the ordinary citizen from all angles these days: Europe or not Europe, Tory or Labour, whipping or a more gentle approach, NHS or private, and so on. Our opinions are canvassed even if no action will be taken.

Even more questions are being asked of the faithful church-goer: traditional or something new, Rome or Church of England, male or female priesthood, diocesan or flying bishop, homo- or hetero-sexual.

For the clergy there is the further problem of finding a new church structure which will ensure that the traditional faith will be preserved without leaving a minority high and dry. Too hasty and drastic solutions may isolate the faithful even more.

As the prophet Joel says, *Multitudes in the valley of decision* – and some answers must be given.

Except the Lord

At this time, it is well to remember the Lord's own words about building on a firm foundation and not on sand. He knew because he was not only a carpenter but possibly a builder as well, if we correctly understand the Greek word. For there are priests and lay people trying to rebuild an ecclesial community governed by orthodox bishops and continuing the Catholic faith and practice which has come down to us through the ages. It is all too easy, however, to play about with structures and to forget what they are meant to promote. It is not enough to offer a safe haven for those sheltering from religious deviations: it is not even enough to say that this haven offers the true faith of our Lord Jesus Christ for we have been so long without learning about that Lord that we no longer understand the message he brought to this world from His Father. These may seem harsh words but consider how the situation could be otherwise.

Faulty foundation

Before the Second World War, five years were required for the training of a priest: three years at university and two years at a theological college. During these years ordinands were first shown the discipline of scholarship and then taught to apply it to all areas of Christian theology, especially the holy scripture. Devotion to our Lord was balanced by learning what our Gospels told us about him: the historical evidence, what manner of man he was, how he fitted into the religious history of Israel. The four Gospels were seen as material for an ever-expanding band of preachers who from the very beginning had both to proclaim and explain the risen Lord.

There was, it is true, a rising swell of critical scholarship which was both sceptical about the Lord's divinity and the authority of the revelation which he brought and also about the reliability of the gospel documents. However, on the whole except in liberal colleges they were treated as nothing more than unproved speculation.

After the war, this conservative and balanced New Testament scholarship was continued but gradually speculation turned into definite theories. Commentaries like Nineham's *St Mark* took a late date for the composition of the Gospels and attributed some of their teaching to the reflections of a later generation. In other words the ministry of our Lord no longer depended on the careful record of eye witness. St John's Gospel was dismissed as a very late piece of writing.

Unfortunately these theories, still unproved, infiltrated most pre-ordination studies except in the definite evangelical colleges and made way for the doubts about the Virgin Birth and the physical resurrection of Jesus. So from the 1960s onwards most of our clergy, including bishops, have been trained in liberal New Testament ideas. This has included Catholic priests who were able to shrug off doubts about the historical Jesus because they had the Jesus of faith in the Mass and sacraments. But, a decision to accept Jesus as Lord cannot be made without historical evidence otherwise it becomes a mere ideology or ideal. A knowledge of our Lord's plans for His Church is essential in a controversy about women priests for nowhere in the Gospels can support for them be found. Ah! say the advocates of a female priesthood, we cannot know what were His wishes because the Gospels were composed by a later generation and by then much of Jesus' actual teaching was fudged by being handed down mostly orally. They have a point here. If a later generation could create its own version of the ministry of Jesus, so can later generations. This has happened in our day.

If we are not to go down the road of further liberalism, we must look again at the other side of the story and ask whether, in a cultured and literate world, the first witnesses of the works and words of Jesus depended only on the unreliable means of oral communication. We shall find that there has always been a scholarship which is better informed.

A well-educated community

At the time of our Lord's birth, the civilising influence of the Greeks was two hundred years old and had penetrated Jewish daily life. A citizen of Palestine would have needed to know a smattering at least of Greek and Latin as well as Hebrew/Aramaic. In the case of a civil servant like Matthew or Levi this would have been essential if he was to satisfy his foreign masters. A high standard for recording history is found in writers like Thucydides who lived and wrote over four hundred years before Christ. Shorthand had long been in use – oxygraphy or tachygraphy, quick writing. The Psalmist also knew about this technique when he refers to the pen of a 'ready' writer (Ps. 45). The Romans developed speedwriting in the first century BC and Cicero mentions it in 63 BC.

In view of the importance of the written word throughout the New Testament it is inconceivable that all known techniques would not have been used in handing on the priceless facts of revelation brought by God's son. New converts would have needed more information about a Master they may never have seen or heard. Teachers and preachers would certainly have needed aide-mémoires for from the first Pentecost onwards the Church was intent on proclaiming the good news about Jesus to an ever-widening audience. This is not to deny a certain amount of editorship in the final product but as Professor Charles Moule has written, those Christians knew the difference between the pre-resurrection situation and the post-resurrection situation and it was their aim to try to tell faithfully the story of how the former led to the latter. In fact they succeeded better than is often allowed.

Clearing away the rubble

Theological speculation is no longer contained within university walls but often is given the freedom of TV and radio. Religious matters are regularly debated with that inclusive ending which is characteristic of the media today. Scholars can be seen theologising on the screen, casting doubts on the most treasured facts of Christian faith, including the authority of Jesus. Documentaries and plays have taken advantage of this uncertainty by introducing fiction, even caricature, into religious productions. Jesus is paired off with Mary Magdalene and dismisssed as a failed revolutionary, a mistaken and bewildered guru or worse. It is worth considering the effect of all this on the British public, even churchgoers who, inside and outside church, have never been taught the other side of the story.

Some scholars, however, have refused to be swept away by the tide of such irresponsible and liberal speculation and one, at least, has said it is time to sweep away a vast amount of dead wood of views which have never been tenable. It is urgent that those holding the Catholic integrity should put the record straight now and include a programme of sound New Testament teaching in plans for the furture. The fact is, liberalism has left us with a faded image of our Lord. Few recognise this because Bible Studies have not been high on our priorities. We have thought that the Sunday gospel reading is sufficient to keep our people in touch with the Jesus of history. These unconnected readings however can only be understood against the background of the whole gospel, otherwise they are isolated pieces of advice. The Gospels are more than this. For example, it is not realised how much of our Lord's work was concerned with sin and its treatment and to ignore this in our lives is to be incomplete Catholics. We are content to allow the media to take over the office of confessor and judge when the sins which are troubling society can only be treated by our Lord, through the confessional.

The Psalms warn us that 'Except the Lord builds the house, their labour is but lost who build it', yet just as a river which loses contact with its source stagnates and disappears we appear to have lost touch with the true Lord of the whole gospel. Unless we take a professional approach to New Testament studies now, we shall be trying to rebuild without an infrastructure, and that is not good architecture.

Printed in the United Kingdom
by Lightning Source UK Ltd.
128744UK00001B/91-210/P

9 780852 446218